Otherworlds

STUDIES IN CORNISH LANGUAGE AND CULTURE

Volume 6

STUDIES IN CORNISH LANGUAGE AND CULTURE
Volume 6

Otherworlds

*Images of Transformation
in Cornish Culture*

Brendan McMahon

evertype

2016

Published by Evertype, 19A Corso Street, Dundee, DD2 1DR, Scotland. *www.evertype.com.*

First edition 2016. Reprinted October 2021.

A catalogue record for this book is available from the British Library.

ISBN-10 1-78201-187-0
ISBN-13 978-1-78201-187-3

ISSN 2753-1597

Typeset in Baskerville by Michael Everson.

Cover design by Michael Everson, based on a photograph "Three of the Nine Stones of Alternun" by Jim Champion, 2007.

Contents

Acknowledgements

Thanks are due to the editors of *Pendragon*, *The Journal of Critical Psychology, Counselling and Psychotherapy*, and *An Baner Kernewek*, in which some of this material first appeared.

Thanks again to Owen McKnight at The Celtic Library, Jesus College, Oxford for his generous help, and to Chris Worth for all her patience and hard work.

Foreword

Joseph Campbell's ground-breaking work, *The Hero with a Thousand Faces* (1949), defined for a generation how comparative mythology could unlock the journey of the individual. His work went on to influence a number of writers, storytellers, and film-makers; among these, most famously. George Lucas, and his development of the *Star Wars* legendarium, from 1977 onwards. Campbell's analysis drew on a variety of sources and demonstrates that important myths from around the world (which have survived for thousands of years) all share a fundamental structure.

It is curious how such an influential idea, expanded and developed by other theorists, has not yet been fully applied onto any of the Celtic territories. Considering their fundamental association with myth and narrative in various forms, it would appear they are ripe for such academic treatment. In this volume, we see one such observer, who dares for the first time to make an application of this awareness of the influence of myth and narrative related to the territory of Cornwall. That observer is Brendan McMahon, and his chosen territory is one that is a highly productive area to consider, for Cornwall has had a very distinctive cultural history.

McMahon, in very many senses, is helping to define this field, but also he is no stranger to it. He has published a series of articles and books over the past few decades—among them his recently published *A Wreck Upon the Ocean: Cornish Folklore in the Age of the Industrial Revolution* (Evertype, 2015) and *Gathering the Fragments: Storytelling and Cultural Resistance in Cornwall* (Evertype, 2016). McMahon has come to offer some radical new theories and make some insightful conclusions about the way in which story is used in Cornish Culture. His skills, in terms of psychoanalytical criticism and extant mythologies and folktales, make him uniquely qualified for this work.

Fundamentally, he has suggested that the particular need for *story* in Cornwall (whether mythological, dramatic, or narrative) is a key indicator of cultural resistance. In this way, stories are touchstones into survival and resilience against a stronger and more powerful neighbour, in the form of England and Englishness. He argues that despite methods of assimilation, difference continues to remain in the twenty-first century, and shows little sign of disappearing or falling away. This mythology, however, has a long history.

In this new volume McMahon delves further into how various transformations have occurred in Cornish culture, showing the reader that fundamental narratives have remained, even though they mutate and reform for new generations. His term for this— "Otherworlds"—indicates a place which facilitates this change and allows for the mechanisms of transformation to be applied. The book here is chock-full of them, and shows how many threads of on-going narrative can be related back to origin myths, heroic narrative, romance, and to the lives of saints. These, it is argued, are the narratives that continue to mingle and merge through our con-temporary culture. The transformation, McMahon maintains, has sometimes not even been noticed by those observing, though here we see the author begin to untangle this knot of interrelationships and connections.

A key theory comes early on in the volume where McMahon reconsiders the Arthurian mythos in Cornwall, particularly in the light of the discovery of the miracle play. *Bewnans Ke [The Life of Saint Ke]*. This text, discovered only in 2000, offers the mythologist several layers of enquiry, and the one which McMahon focuses upon is the figure of Ke himself. Ke was a British saint, who in the drama, assists not only in the defeat of a local tyrant (named Teudar) but also engages with much Arthurian matter. In the play, Arthur is faced with the threat of the Roman Empire, but then has to deal with the rebellion of his nephew Mordred. It is Ke who steps in as the peace negotiator between Mordred and Arthur. Maybe, McMahon argues, Ke is the central myth who later constitutes the figure of Kay who is constructed in the later embellishments of this narrative. This is the fundamental kind of transformation that the author considers here. The play of St Ke has also reinforced our theatrical knowledge of

Cornwall from the Medieval period, and has shown how earlier myth was recycled for use in those dramas. Thus McMahon sets up a paradox of cultural plundering for the next generation's method of resistance.

Saints themselves and the recycling of hagiography form a core part of the argument here. The individuality of the cult of saints in Cornwall is examined, and it is suggested that for those accommodating and assimilating Cornwall, the concern and fixation upon saints was a way in which Cornish distinctiveness persisted. This was not only through the dramas—such as *Beunans Meriasek [The Life of Meriasek]* and the aforementioned *Beunans Ke* —but the whole cultural geography that existed in the territory. Obviously there have been lost layers of myth (as well as a considerable loss of texts) but the persistence of this ideology of place has remained. Now, saints are held less by Cornish people in terms of their religiosity (the place is now, like most other territories in Europe, resoundingly secular), although the awareness of the shaping and significance of the saints on place and people is still ingrained into the Cornish consciousness. Therefore, we may conclude that a number of transformations have taken place, running from indigenous, pagan, and pre-Christian local deity, to Christianized saint and community founder, to then symbol of identity and resistance within wider Anglicization and globalization. When one realizes this, one begins to understand the transformative value of myth, and also why certain myths survive, and indeed evolve.

One further myth of is of great interest to Cornish scholars: that of the figure of Joseph of Arimathea, to whom McMahon rightly pays considerable attention here. A figure in the second and third surviving plays of *Ordinalia*, Joseph was not only a key figure in the Biblical narrative, but in Cornwall also had his own mythology built around him. Joseph may well have accompanied the boy Christ to Cornwall in his role as a tin trader (a trade to the eastern Mediterranean that we know existed from the archaeology found at Tintagel) and then may have brought a thorn from Christ's crown back to Glastonbury (also of course, the last resting place of King Arthur). This myth was very important to the Cornish, not only because it connected them to the greatest story every told (that of

Christ's death and resurrection) but also their place within the wider narrative. Joseph again therefore is a transformative figure, whose "Otherworld" qualities linked the present to a key moment in the mythological past. The fact that tin mining continued to be important in Cornwall for a thousand years or more only reinforced the original myth.

Support for McMahon's analysis may be found elsewhere. Bernard Deacon, in his recent work, *Cornwall's First Golden Age: From Arthur to the Normans* (2016), challenges the usual historical and literary criticism of Cornwall from the sixth to the eleventh centuries, arguing the contrary to some previous observers, that Cornwall's assimilation into England was more or less complete by the end of the eleventh century. He finds plenty of evidence to support the fact that a distinctive, culturally and politically aware Cornwall remained in place a good deal longer. As part of his narrative, Deacon— although admitting that there were limitations for the royal patronage of bardic or poetic myth—also asserts that literary, and therefore, mythological production, continued a long time into the early medieval period. Some of the myths considered by McMahon were obviously transformed in this period, and then further transformed in the high Medieval period. It might even be that the lack of centralized royal patronage contributed to the devolved way in which later drama developed in Cornwall. Deacon's observations on the non-assimilation of Cornwall in the early period, alongside McMahon's reading of myth (originating in the same period), make for a new understanding of the way in which early Cornwall evolved. Both works also offer a context for the initial shaping and transformation of myth in the territory.

McMahon's endeavour here will upset several apple-carts of previous understandings of the way in which culture transforms and develops. But this is fine. Occasionally, we need people like him to come along, who are daring enough to scatter the apples everywhere and begin to reassemble the pieces. The cultural "Avalon" needs digging into, and needs to be better understood. Many observers are in the process of a wider reassessment of Cornwall's position within the cultural landscape of both these islands and the rest of the European continent. In this way, we are peeling back some of the film that coats the lens through which we see and understand Cornish culture. At the end of the day, there will be no final truth, but works such as this, help us to come all the closer to it.

Alan M. Kent
Probus, 2016

Introduction

Stories

We all live by stories, though we don't always know what they are. Stories explain who we are and how we got to be the way we are. They can be used therapeutically for instance to help us understand ourselves better, and to recapture parts of the self which have been lost. We become a part of our family and community stories when we are born, and help to shape those stories. Our part in those stories is shaped by what has gone before, though we do have choices about where we take them and how we change them in response to a changing world. We use our stories to position ourselves in space and time and to give our lives meaning.

At the highest level we do this by using stories to align ourselves with what we conceive to be the ultimate spiritual or philosophical truths about the human condition. These stories link us to other people who share our beliefs, and together we construct a common culture based on our shared beliefs (a story in which only I could believe would be a psychosis). Such stories frequently embody profound truths about how human beings think and feel and relate to each other, which explains their power to move us and to endure for a very long time: it is sometimes dismissively said for instance that folk stories were mere entertainment and of course they did provide some distraction in lives that were often unimaginably hard. But hard-working people do not have time to waste. Storytelling was adaptive: it helped to bind people together and make sense of the world.

Within a particular culture, stories can link up to form an integrated system linking past and present, individual and communal, material and spiritual. Though this wider paradigm is not usually held by any one person at any particular time, it is implicit and shapes the beliefs and behaviour of the community. Many traditional societies held a similar construct, though industrialism and colonization have destroyed or fragmented it almost everywhere.

But the fragments can still be pieced together to give some sense of the original pattern, itself a kaleidoscope which changes over time. In Cornwall for instance, the story of Béroul's *Tristan and Iseult* is firmly set in a Cornish landscape which can be traced to this day. That story is also part of the Arthurian legend, and parallels the Arthur/Medraut/Guinevere triad, whose climax is also set in Cornwall. It also echoes the mysterious conception of Arthur at Tintagel, and other stories of conflicting love and loyalty in the wider Celtic world, especially Ireland, as we shall see. Indeed, links between Cornwall and the other Celtic-speaking countries play a significant part in Cornish culture; the saints of Cornwall seem always to be en route between Wales, Ireland, Cornwall, and Brittany.[1] Their supernatural means of transport (St Piran reached Cornwall from Ireland by floating on a millstone) underlines their otherworldly character and connects them with the eremitical tradition, which was especially important in Celtic Christianity, as do their frequent miracles, identifying them with the healing power of Christ.

In yet another story Christ himself visits Cornwall with his mother, the Blessed Virgin Mary and uncle, St Joseph of Arimathea, who was himself connected with the foundation of Glastonbury Abbey where he was believed to be buried. It is less widely known that both Christ and St Joseph were credited with the discovery and first smelting of tin, an event of crucial economic and social importance for Cornish history. A different origin story for tin is told in the "Tom the Tinkeard" droll in Hunt's *Popular Romances of the West of England*. For Christian Cornwall the Holy Visit of Christ connects land and people with the scriptural account of his life, death and resurrection, for believers the most important of all stories in their world, which is the subject of the *Ordinalia*, the dramatic trilogy which marks the high point of Middle Cornish literature. These plays were performed publicly at dozens of sites in west Cornwall. The sites themselves

1   Doble, G. H. (1997 reprint). The Saints of Cornwall I-VI. Felinfach Llanerch.

seem often to be ancient burial mounds, already rich in association with Cornwall's past, and it seems likely from parish records that many local people were involved in the productions. The surviving plays (and many have been lost) seem all to have been written at Glasney College in Penryn, one of a number of Cornish religious foundations dissolved after the English Reformation. As Cornwall was increasingly absorbed into the Tudor nation-state Glasney and its Cornish drama at first played an important part in its cultural resistance, though a series of rebellions beginning late in the fifteenth century offered a more formidable opposition to English hegemony.

Arthur and the Saints

Out of Glasney too came a number of saints' plays, of which two survive, the *Beunans Meriasek* or "Life of Meriasek" and *Bewnans Ke*, the "Life of St Kea". Though these plays are part of a hagiographic tradition which is found right across Europe, they do contain specifically Cornish features. "Beunans Meriasek" emphasizes the saint's connections with Camborne but also his Breton origins. Philip Payton has argued that the play is "a subversive document", a vehicle for Cornish identity because of its treatment of "Teudar" the "foreign tyrant", which may represent Cornish hostility to the monarchy around the time of the Flamank/An Gof rising in 1497.

St Kea too has to contend with a heathen tyrant called Teudar. He too performs healing miracles like Christ and lays foundations for the Christian communities of the future. The missing folios in the manuscript make it difficult to follow his further adventures, and much of what remains is taken up with King Arthur's conflict with the Roman Emperor Lucius. It is difficult to grasp how these plots fit together, given the state of the manuscript. In the *Concise Oxford Dictionary of English Place Names*, Crowall asserts that "Ke is identical with Kei and goes back to the earlier Cai".[2] These early Welsh/British heroes were the originals for "Kay the Seneschal" in the later Arthurian romances, though the character changes from hero to curmudgeon, and it is of course impossible to speak of one stable personality underlying all these literary incarnations, which may ultimately be rooted in Celtic myth. His name "Cai" is early

---

2   See discussion in Gowans, L. M. (1988). *Cei and the Arthurian Legend. Arthurian Studies XVIII.* Cambridge, D. S. Brewer.

Welsh derived from the Latin "Caius", and it occurs in several place-names such as Gwryr Cei and Caer Gai. His earliest appearance in the Welsh poem "Pa gur" places him in a mythological context to which there are Irish analogues. He is shown fighting nine hags "on the uplands of Ystafngwn" and going to Mona to fight Palug's cat, a mysterious otherworldly beast. In this poem too, though the hero is mostly seen in a north British setting, he is also associated with Cornwall:

> "Cai entreated them as he hewed them down
> When Celli was lost men endured savagery
> Cai mocked them as he cut them down."[3]

"Celli" or Kelliwig is frequently referred to as Arthur's Cornish centre of operations, though the battle referred to in this early and often obscure poem is unclear. Cei's close relations with Arthur are emphasized in many Arthurian romances, and they do seem to date back to early times: according to one tradition he and Arthur were foster-brothers. This branch of the story certainly does predate the medieval romances since it reflects the ancient Celtic practice of fosterage by which a son was brought up in the home of a powerful, unrelated patron. The foster father would take responsibility for the child's upbringing from the age of seven years, and their relationship constituted a special bond.[4] In the Irish story of Cú Chulainn the leading men of Ulster compete over who is to be the boy hero's foster father. The Cú's relationship with his foster brother Ferdiad is particularly close and this heightens the sense of tragic irony when the two are forced to fight.[5]

If Cei and Arthur are connected in this way then they are especially close. If Kea and Cei are the "same" person (and it is of course difficult to say quite what this means), then it goes some way to explaining their juxtaposition in the Cornish play, which is otherwise unexplained. But they are presented as contemporaries,

3   *Ibid.*, pp. 4-6.
4   See MacKillop, J. (1998). *Dictionary of Celtic Mythology*. Oxford, Oxford University Press, p. 213.
5   For the story see Kinsella, T. (1970). *The Tain*. London, Oxford University Press. And Carson, C. (2007). *The Tain*. London, Penguin.

which must have made sense to a Cornish audience. In Albert Le Grand's "Life of St Kea", Ke attempts to mediate between Arthur and "Modredus", his nephew, in order to make peace and keep out Childeric's pagan Saxons, but his efforts are thwarted and he is forced to return to Brittany. Mediation was a role expected of the early Celtic saints, and this incident may be historic. Saint Ronan is on his way to Mag Rath to prevent battle there when Suibhne hinders him and is cursed in punishment:

"His fingers were palsied, his feet trembled, his heart beat quick, his senses were overcome, his sight was distorted, his weapons fell naked from his hands, so that through Ronan's curse he went like a bird of the air in madness and imbecility."[6]

Other saints in the Celtic world also intervene to avert conflict, though their efforts are rarely successful. The story of Ke's attempt to mediate and unify the British Celts against the Saxon invaders may have been known in Cornwall, as it evidently was in Brittany, though it does not appear in the surviving text of the play, and would have strengthened the association between Ke and Arthur, providing the unifying factor which is missing from *Bewnans Ke* as we have it.

Apart from these links between Kea and Arthur there are other hints that the early saints were seen as transitional figures linking the Arthurian resistance to Saxon invasion with the Cornwall which emerged from British Dumnonia and its cultural resistance throughout the Middle Ages. The great saint Petroc for instance, who gave his name to Padstow, is mentioned in the Welsh triads as one of the few men who survived the Battle of Camlann, fighting with Arthur against Modred and his Saxon allies. In later life he also (like Ke and Meriasek) is opposed to "Teudor, a cruel and fierce man who oppresses the people".[7]

It is difficult to be certain, but it would seem that the early saints took on a symbolic role as founders and guardians of the Cornish communities after the catastrophe of Camlann. It is difficult to be certain because:

---

6   O'Keefe, J. G. (1913). *Buile Suibne: Being the Adventures of Suibhne Geilt, A Middle Irish Romance*. London, Irish Texts Society.

7   Doble, G. H., *op. cit.*, V, Four, p. 142.

During the Reformation and the succeeding centuries of indifference, all the written lives of the patron saints of Cornish parishes were deliberately or negligently destroyed,

though fortunately

> in Brittany there was no Reformation and so numerous lives of Cornish saints which have disappeared entirely in Cornwall (though some of them were written there), have been preserved in Breton manuscripts.[8]

Of course stories about the saints could only have acquired an anti-Tudor resonance a thousand years after their own lifetimes, but if they were already associated with Cornish identity and cultural resistance that would perhaps make them more available as appropriate channels for Cornish feeling in the atmosphere of 1497 and after. Apart from the suppression of the saints *Lives*, attempts were made in the later Middle Ages to replace Cornish church dedications with saints from the universal church, to remove their distinctive Cornish associations, which does suggest that the English ecclesiastical authorities were suspicious of the Cornish saints and of the veneration in which Cornish communities held them. That saints plays commemorating them, plays in which they were still being portrayed as the opponents of "foreign tyrants" were still being staged a thousand years on, attests to their central place in Cornish culture. Their links with the Arthurian resistance, though tenuous as we have them, may once have been stronger, and they later acquired roots in folklore which became an important expression of Cornish identity, especially after the demise of the language.

Folklore and the Future

After the deliberate destruction of the language and of the institutions which had sustained it, the voice of Cornwall could only be heard in the traditional stories of the droll tellers, at least until its writers found a new voice in English fiction and verse where its distinctive tones were not always so easy to hear. But still the folktale

8   *Ibid.*, p. 132.

helped the audience to come together to celebrate their identity and make sense of their own world, increasingly distorted by the irresistible forces of early capitalism, through the lens of the otherworldly stories. Increasingly Arthur belonged less and less to Cornwall as he was pressed into the service of the British imperial project, and his place in folklore was restricted to place names and literary references, at least until he was reclaimed by language revivalists at the end of the nineteenth century. Otherworlds can provide us with escapist fantasies as some of the Cornish stories do, or they can be laboratories in which we can test our assumptions about the world and perhaps change it.

The story of Tristan and Iseult likewise left little trace in Cornish folklore. That the story once existed in a Cornish form is probable, judging from the accurate topography of Béroul's twelfth-century French version, but it is futile to seek for an "original" for a story with so ancient and universal a theme. The form of the hero's name given on the famous "Tristan Stone" appears to be Pictish, even if it does refer to the Tristan in the story, which is puzzling: there are strong arguments too for a northern origin for the Arthurian legends. But such arguments miss the point. Narrative tradition in Britain was fragmented by the Anglo-Saxon invasions, and these traditions must have taken many developmental paths as Britain broke up into separate kingdoms as its former unity was lost: since the Britons of Wales, Strathclyde and the Southwest were one when these stories took shape (though they may ultimately be even older than that), it makes little sense to argue about origins. This may also explain the paucity of place names related to the Tristan story, in comparison with the parallel story of Diarmuid, Gráinne, and Fionn, which has left traces all over the landscape of Ireland and the Scottish Highlands.[9] But there can be no doubt that Cornwall played an important part in the development of the stories of Arthur, and of Tristan, Mark, and Iseult before they became part of the wider European heritage in the twelfth century.

This aspect of Cornish culture, its ability to reach out and connect with a wider European heritage is largely unknown and unrecognized in England. The international activity of the saints, the seminal

9   See Ni Sheaghdha, N. (ed) (1967). *Tor Vigheacht Dhiarmada Agus Ghrainne: The Pursuit of Diarmid and Grainne*. Dublin, Irish Texts Society.

importance of Arthur's story in European literature, and its Cornish provenance, the reflection of the Tristan/Iseult/Mark story in the geographical triad Cornwall/Ireland/Brittany (there are actually two triads if you include the unfortunate Iseult of the White Hands) have all been lost. In Cornwall itself the awareness of fellowship with the other Celtic nations, especially Brittany, has lingered however. But Cornwall has always looked beyond that too, to the Europe whose religion it shared, and later to the wider world, to Australia, California and South Africa, where its people went in search of a livelihood denied to them at home. Paradoxically, it has been when Cornwall was most itself, in the Cornish language drama, that it was most in touch with the European mainstream. Conversely the more Cornish writers looked to English models, as the Bosons did in the late seventeenth and early eighteenth centuries, the less they had to say both to their own people and to the outside world. In their long captivity the Cornish dreamed of another world in which their distinctive voice could be heard and they could take their place among the nations of Europe. Like other revolutionary visions this was also an attempt to recreate or re-imagine the past.

The revivalists at the turn of the nineteenth century were certainly aware of the importance of both the language and the Arthurian legend in shaping a new national consciousness, as we shall see. The nineteenth century had already seen attempts to collect and publish what remained of Cornish literature and folklore in the service of the imperial project, but this material then became available to the Cornish themselves to help them articulate a vision of a very different world. And the language of Arthurian symbolism was also to play a part in this vision. The imperial project itself is now long dead and it may be that an Arthur for our times will at last be able to realize his libertarian potential in a postmodern, perhaps fragmenting Britain. In the 1980s a Farnborough biker, believing himself to be King Arthur *redivivus* changed his name to Arthur Uther Pendragon and became an environmental civil rights activist, campaigning for improved access to Stonehenge. Though often mocked by the media, he has been described as:

an intelligent and adroit operator of political performance art. He activated the myth of the sleeping hero who will awake when his people has need of him, and turned it against an alliance of government and big business which seemed to him to have acquired the status of a menacing and alien power.[10]

Though this is perhaps not less of an appropriation of the Cornish Arthur than the earlier one, it does at least illustrate the king's emancipatory strength. As I write this (in 2016) we live in less hopeful times, and it may seem that challenging power is impossible, on the basis of an ancient story at least: but Arthur's story is not over yet, nor is his power to move the hearts of men and women. For over fifteen hundred years, in Peter Korrel's words, it has been true that "every author uses the Arthurian legend to suit his own purposes".[11] Some of these purposes have been unworthy of him. But he may still possess the power to challenge "menacing and alien power" as he did briefly in his own lifetime.

The Arthurian legend particularly illustrates the interconnectedness of the culture, stretching from ancient times to the present, changing shape in response to history and the changing needs of the people, and the story of the sleeping hero exemplifies this, so Arthur of Cornwall was transformed into a European then global embodiment of chivalry and an ideal moral code, and Tristan and Iseult was changed from a grim Iron Age triad into an ideal of romantic love. Even some of the humbler folktales have gone global: the story of Jack the Giant-killer seems to have originated in Cornwall.[12]

10   Hutton, R. (2003). *Witches, Druids and King Arthur*. London, Bloomsbury, pp. 252-3.
11   Korrel, P. (1984). *An Arthurian Triangle: A Study of the Origin, Development and Characterisation of Arthur, Guinevere and Moared*. Leiden, E. J. Brill.
12   See Deane, T. and Shaw, T. (2003). *Folklore of Cornwall*. Stroud, Tempus.

Chapter 1

The Holy Visit

And did those feet?

At the beginning of the nineteenth century the great English mystic William Blake wrote a poem in two books entitled "Milton". In this complicated poem Blake explores his own complicated response to the author of *Paradise Lost* and pictures Milton's descent to earth to save the world through the power of imagination. The poem culminates in a vision of Christ in which he "went and walked forth / From Felpham's Vale clothed in clouds of blood". Blake loathed the new industrial civilization of his time, the "dark satanic mills" which he considered an offence against nature and the human spirit, along with the repressive aspects of the state and of the state religion, and looked to the second coming of Christ as a metaphor for redemption and transformation.

The well-known preface to "Milton" begins with the famous lines:

> "And did those feet in ancient time
> Walk upon England's mountains green?"

which have been sung at countless Cup Finals and Last Nights. Though many people who sing it are dimly aware of legends that Christ visited these shores as a boy, few are aware that the legends locate him in Cornwall, and with specific locations within Cornwall. In an undated early twentieth century pamphlet the Reverend H. A. Lewis writes of oral traditions linking Christ to Marazion and Ding Dong in Penwith, St Day and Falmouth, Saint Just in Roseland, Lammana and Looe Island in Wivelshire, and further tells us that "these are all either tin districts or adjacent havens".[13] This link with

---
13 For this and what follows see Lewis, H. A. (nd). *Christ in Cornwall?* Falmouth, J. H. Lake.

the tin trade recurs frequently within the somewhat fragmented tradition.

Another clerical enthusiast, the Rev. C. C. Dobson identified four independent traditions:

1. The boy Jesus was brought by Joseph of Arimathea to Cornwall, where Jesus taught him how to extract tin.
2. Joseph and Jesus came to Somerset and stayed at a place called Paradise.
3. Joseph and Jesus stayed in the Mendips, at a place called Priddy.
4. Joseph and Jesus visited Glastonbury, which may be the same as "Paradise", where they built the famous "wattle church", which burned down in the Middle Ages. Old maps give the area around Burnham the name of "Paradise", and according to Dobson there was a Paradise House and a Paradise Farm in the locality.[14]

The old British name for Glastonbury, "Ynys Avalon" or "The Isle of Apples", signified the Otherworld, the equivalent of the biblical Paradise.

The legend certainly links Glastonbury with Cornwall in a number of ways. "Lammana" for instance was a tiny priory of Glastonbury Abbey before the Conquest. Arthur, the legendary king of Cornwall has a grave in the grounds of the Abbey, though this may well be a monastic fraud to enhance the status of the Abbey. But its existence does suggest that such a connection would have been credible in medieval times. Joseph of Arimathea, linked to Cornwall through the tin trade, planted his staff at the Abbey, where is blossomed as the famous Glastonbury thorn which is still to be found there. Whatever else it may contain, the story does provide an explanation for the origins of Christianity in Britain, at a time when that process was not clearly understood. Cornwall is therefore linked in legendary history at least with one of the most important events in British history.[15] William of Malmesbury tells us that the "old church was

14 Dobson, C. C. (1936). *Did Our Lord Visit Britain as they say in Cornwall and Somerset?* Glastonbury, Avalon Press.
15 Thomas, C. (1981). *Christianity in Roman Britain. London*, B. T. Batsford, p. 42.

built by Joseph of Arimathea" who came to Britain with his followers "sixty three years from the Incarnation of the Lord and fifteen from the Assumption of the Blessed Mary when they began faithfully to preach the faith of Christ".[16] Though he records many miracles and the visits of saints and kings, William recounts no legends of the boy Jesus. He himself never even mentions Joseph, references to whom were interpolated by later writers.

In 1899 Sabine Baring-Gould linked this story to Cornwall in his *Book of Cornwall*:

> And the Cornish story to the effect that Joseph of Arimathea came in a boat to Cornwall, and brought the child Jesus with him, and the latter taught him how to extract the tin and purge it of its wolfram.[17]

Baring-Gould also tells the better-known story that tin was discovered by Saint Piran, but the story of the Holy Visit is clearly much older than Baring-Gould's own time, even if evidence is scarce. St Jesus Well in Miniver was famous for centuries because its water was said to be a cure for whooping cough.[18] It was commonly said in St Just in Lewis's day that "Joseph of Arimathea and Our Lord came in a boat and anchored in St Just creek", and that "forty years previously it was as much as your life was worth" to express any doubt that Christ came to St Just.[19] Many pointed to a curiously marked stone upon which Christ was said to have stepped when he landed, and at Falmouth it was said that "Joseph of Arimathea landed at the Strand, crossed the stream, and went up Smithick Hill", a comment which only makes sense in terms of a local topography which vanished long ago.[20] At Chacewater it was said that Jesus and Joseph "worked at Creeg Brawse", an ancient tin-mine near St Day, and an old lady Lewis knew told him: "Of course

16 William of Malmesbury (1908 reprint). *The Antiquities of Glastonbury*. Felinfach, Llanerch, pp. 3-4.

17 Baring Gould, S. (1899). *A Book of Cornwall*. London, Methuen, p. 57.

18 See Courtney, M. A. (1886, reprint 1998). *Cornish Feasts and Folklore*. Penzance, Oakmagic, p. 64.

19 Lewis, *op. cit.*, pp. 4-6.

20 *Ibid.*, p. 5.

we know Our Saviour preached to the miners. He was very fond of the miners."[21] The song "Joseph was a Tin-man" was well known in the Redruth district, and was revived in the twentieth century by Steeleye Span.

In Penwith it was believed that Christ visited the ancient Ding-Dong mine, and he was said to have made land in Mount's Bay at Looe Island. A common thread is the widespread belief that Joseph had strong connections with the mining community, based on the miners' curious whispered invocation, "Joseph was in the tin-trade". This invocation is said to have persisted into recent times. The Cornish tin trade certainly has very early origins:

> The Irish "copper age" ended about 2100 B.C. with the rapid transition to the use of time-bronze, the tin most likely coming from Cornwall, a peninsula that lies conveniently astride the maritime routes between Brittany and southwest Ireland.[22]

That Joseph of Arimathea came to Cornwall for tin is feasible. In around 320 BCE Pytheas of Massalia sailed around Britain, and may have bought Cornish tin which was much in demand in the ancient world.[23]

The smelting of tin was of huge importance in Cornish life, and various legendary explanations of how it first came about are given. Apart from the story that Christ taught the skill to Joseph, we have the attractive tale of St Piran, who floated over from Ireland on a millstone. One day while cooking a meal he used a large slab of black stone as a hearth; as the fire grew hotter he saw a stream of pure white tin flowing from the flames. When he told the local people they celebrated, and this was the origin of the Piran's Day Feast, which continued well into the nineteenth century. St Piran was a drinking man, and is supposed to have died drunk: his feast was celebrated with carnivalesque exuberance by the mining community.[24]

---

21 *Ibid.*, p. 7.
22 Cunliffe, B. (2011). *Europe between the Oceans. 9000 B. C. – A. D. 1000.* New Haven, Yale University Press, p. 208.
23 *Ibid.*, p. 7.
24 Courtney, *op. cit.*, p. 67.

One of the longest surviving drolls is Hunt's story of "Tom the Tinkeard". Among its many episodes is a story entitled "How Tom and the Tinkeard found the Tin, and how it led to Morva Fair:[25]

> Tom and his friend Jack the Tinkeard had a wrestling match followed by a game of quoits. Tom's third throw was so strong that it cut a great hole in the bank, exposing a mass of black and grey stone. Tom didn't know what tin was, but Jack did:
>
> "Why Tom," says Jack, "thee art a made man. If these banks are all tin there is enough here to buy all the land and all the houses from sea to sea."[26]

Tom said that as he didn't know how to dress tin it was of no use to him. Jack offered to dress it for the market in return for half-shares. He did so, then Tom took the tin to Marazion, to the mayor, who gave him a good price. The Lord of Pengerswick, who was a wizard, tried to extract the secret of the tin from Jack without success. In the end he tried to stab Jack but was defeated by the Tinkeard's own magic powers.

After many more adventures Jack married Tom's daughter young Jane and they had a great party on a Sunday, which was the origin of Morva Feast. The telling of this story, itself a communal event, commemorates and validates an affirmation of identity, rooted in the past and extending into the future:

> Morvah Feast, which is the nearest Sunday to the 1st August, is said to have been instituted in memory of a wrestling match, throwing of quoits etc, which took place there one Sunday "when there were giants in the land". On the following Monday there was formerly a large fair, and although Morvah is a very small village without any attractions, the farmers flocked to it in great numbers to drink and feast sitting on the hedges of the small fields

25 Hunt, R. (1881 3rd edition). *Popular Romances of the West of England*. London, Chatto and Windus, pp. 66-71.

26 *Ibid.*, p. 67.

common in West Cornwall. "Three on one horse, like going to Morvah Fair" is an old proverb.[27]

All these differing stories of the discovery of tin, however fanciful, are deeply rooted in the experience of the Cornish people, and their sense of who they are. Saint Piran is their patron saint, and his flag representing white tin flowing from the dark Cornish rock, has become a symbol of national renewal. Hunt located his story among the "Romances and Superstitions of the Mythic Ages", specifically in the "Age of the Giants", and tin is also discovered by the mysterious, otherworldly Jack the Tinkeard, whose title identified him with the metal which has played such an important part in Cornish history. He is a "culture bearer" like Lugh in Irish myth, like Piran and Joseph, who comes from a distant land to transmit knowledge and skills, as Prometheus brought the knowledge of fire to the human race. This is of course a mythic event, not an historic one. And Christ's discovery of the white metal, in an alternative version of the story links Cornish history intimately with the sacred history of the death and resurrection, the common heritage of Europe: this link is underlined in the *Ordinalia* plays. The hard lives of the mining communities are transformed by becoming part of the devine plan as Cornwall is changed from a backward English province into an equal participant in the European destiny.

The Holy Grail

Joseph of Arimathea is also connected with the story of the Holy Grail. The meaning of the Grail itself is not easily summarized. Specifically it refers to the cup or dish which was used by Christ at the Last Supper on the night before his crucifixion, and is therefore an object of huge spiritual power and significance, which spawned a large literature in the Middle Ages, in which it became a potent symbol of sanctity. It was said that Joseph of Arimathea had used it to collect the blood of the crucified Christ, and that he subsequently brought it to North Wales.[28] The ten most important versions of the story were written between 1180 and 1230.

27 Courtney, *op. cit.*, pp. 51-2.
28 Drabble, M. (ed.) (2000). *The Oxford Companion to English Literature*. Oxford, O. U. P., p. 425.

The origins of the tale are not clear, but it seems likely that one aspect of it relates to Celtic tradition, and it has been linked with the cauldron, the Celtic symbol of regeneration: famous examples include the Cauldron of Ceridwen which transformed Gwion Bach into Taliesin in the Welsh story, the magic Cauldrons Cú Chulainn brought back from Scotland, and the cauldron of the Irish god the Dagda, one of the Four Treasures of the Tuatha Dé Danann.[29] But however deep this layer of meaning may go, the story of the Grail is predominantly a Christian one. Joseph appears in Robert de Borun's "Joseph" in connection with the Grail, sitting where Christ sat at the Last Supper, where he is commanded by an angel to give the Grail to "Bron" who is to become Master of the Grail. Though "Bron" in this story seems to refer back to the British god Bran the Blessed whose severed head defended Britain from invasion until Arthur ill-advisedly had it dug up, the setting is emphatically Christian.[30] Joseph is here the Guardian of the Grail, and Galahad was said to be his son. In some versions Joseph is himself the "maimed king" who is replaced by the young Kea in what was once believed to be a solar myth. His visit to Cornwall connects the land with Celtic myth, Christian allegory and the great themes of sacrifice and redemption, though the extent to which these connections may have been present in the minds of those who told the story of the Holy Visit may be doubtful. Nonetheless the story can be seen as a way of uniting Cornish culture with wider European concerns, and countering the marginalization imposed in the centuries after Dumnonia's defeat.

St Joseph's connection with the "matere of Britain" is close and detailed. He planted the holy thorn on Wearyall Hill at Glastonbury, a descendant of which still flowers on Christmas Day, and he is buried there close to the supposed grave of Arthur. Like Arthur he had twelve followers, and this also of course identifies him with Christ. In most Celtic lands it is considered unlucky to cut down a hawthorn tree, and an Elizabethan Puritan who tried to cut down the Holy Thorn was magically blinded.[31] In eastern tradition Joseph

29   MacKillop, *op. cit.*, p. 73.
30   Loomis, R. S. (1926, reprint 1993). *Celtic Myth and Arthurian Romance.* London, Constable.
31   See Spence, L. (1948). *The Minor Traditions of British Mythology.* London, Rider

was the uncle of the Blessed Virgin, who was supposed to have accompanied him on his visit to Marazion. Saint Joseph was also said to have been an ancestor of King Arthur, whose body was "discovered" in Glastonbury in 1190.

Saints of Brittany

Another link with Cornwall comes through St Anna, the mother of Mary, There is a Breton tradition that Anna was born in Cornouaille, and that she was brutally treated by her husband. She was then pregnant and, fearing for her unborn child, she sailed away to Palestine with the help of an angel. When she reached Nazareth she gave birth to Mary who at the age of fifteen married the carpenter Joseph, at which point Anna returned to Brittany. There she gave away her property and lived quietly at Palue, where Jesus came to visit her and she eventually died, whereupon her body was assumed into Heaven. At Lammana in Cornwall, which once belonged to Glastonbury Abbey, there was a St Anna's well. This saint was believed to intercede for childless women, and a chapel on the old Looe Bridge was also dedicated to her. Lewis wonders whether the name "Lammana" could originally have been "Llan Anna", the church of Anna. Brittany of course was populated by refugees from Britain following the Anglo-Saxon invasions, and had strong links with Cornwall. Their shared traditions and trade links endured for centuries: King Mark of Cornwall, who plays an important part in the story of "Tristan and Iseult" also held land in Brittany.

It is however possible that the legend of the Mother of the Virgin has become confused with the obscure tradition that the mother of the Breton Saint Samson of Dol was a Welshwoman called Anna. After he became a bishop Samson left Wales and went to Cornwall: Samson is the patron of Golant and Southill in mid-Cornwall. After he left Cornwall he founded the famous monastery at Dol, and his cult spread across the Celtic lands after his death, and as far afield as Switzerland and Italy. His sarcophagus at Dol was visited by pilgrims from Britain and elsewhere. His cult was evidently popular in Cornwall, and a twelfth-century Breton writer tells us that Mark

and Co., p. 103. And Lewis, L. S. (1922). *St. Joseph of Arimathea at Glastonbury*. Wells, Clare and Son, p. 24.

and Iseult worshipped at his church in Golant near Castle Dore. Samson's *Life* is the earliest known Celtic hagiography: he came from an aristocratic Romano-British family in south-eastern Wales, and

> coming from the union of two great families from Demetia and Ventia, Samson was quite representative of the missionary colonisation movement which, originating from these kingdoms, reached Cornwall.[32]

It is not unlikely that the British from Cornwall took these stories with them to Brittany, especially as Childebert the king founded bishoprics for them at Leon and perhaps at Dol.[33] As Lewis says, "all these West of England stories have the same sheen".[34] And so Anna became the patron saint of Brittany, and the Blessed Virgin spent her last days at Glastonbury where she died and was buried, despite traditional Catholic teaching that she was "assumed" into Heaven, along with Joseph himself, as a recognition of their sanctity. We recall that Arthur's passing was similarly ambiguous. Mary in this version may have been buried in the "Ealde Chirche", the old wattle church which Christ himself helped to build.

Joseph in the *Ordinalia*

But Joseph of Arimathea was to reappear at a defining moment in Cornish cultural history, in the *Ordinalia*, a fourteenth century cycle of "mystery plays" in the Cornish language which was probably written at Glasney College and performed at the open-air *Plen an gwary* or "playing places" of which there were once many dotting the west Cornish countryside. Like the Corpus Christi cycles of England and France, the *Ordinalia* begins with the creation of the world, going on to depict the Passion and death of Christ, and finally his Resurrection from the dead. This trilogy is not the only example of drama in the Cornish language that survives from the later Middle Ages: there are also the saints' plays of Kea and Meriasek, and others have undoubtedly been lost. At a time when literacy was rare the

32 Gioc *et al.* (2003). *The British Settlement of Brittany*. Stroud, Tempus, pp. 127-8.
33 Taylor, T. (1925, reprint 1991). *The Life of Saint Samson of Dol*. Felinfach, Llanerch.
34 Lewis, *op. cit.*, p. 41.

mystery plays played an important role in disseminating the Christian faith, and in Cornwall's case in celebrating the language and cultural identity of the people. The "playing places" were often built on ancient burial mounds, embodying the continuity of Cornish history, and Alan Kent believes that:

> the high concentration of dramatic activity in the comparatively small territory of Cornwall may have made for an exchange of ideas, not only with the rest of Britain but also on the Continent.[35]

The *Ordinalia* plays make extensive use of place-names to locate the Gospel story in a local landscape, and this must have increased the sense of dramatic involvement for local audiences. The saints' plays too celebrated the legends of local communities and their religious founders, going back centuries, and must have helped to keep their stories alive across the generations. This was especially so at times when Cornish church dedications were being Anglicized in an attempt to erode Cornish culture.[36]

The story of the death and resurrection of Christ was of course the "big narrative" which bound together the whole of medieval Europe, and Joseph of Arimathea played a big part in it. His story is drawn both from the New Testament account of the Passion and from the so-called Gospel of Nicodemus, the most influential of the apocrypha (that is, texts never accorded a place in the official version of the New Testament sanctioned by the Church), and it is this text which contributed the "Harrowing of Hell", and the "Death of Pilate" to the third Cornish play, the *Resurrexio Domini*.[37] The "Gospel of Nicodemus" contains the story of Joseph's imprisonment by the Jewish people, angry that he had obtained custody of Christ's body and buried it in his own tomb. The Cornish *Resurrexio* alters this

---

35 Kent, A. (2000). *The Literature of Cornwall: Continuity, Identity, Difference 1000-2000.* Bristol, Reccliffe, p. 41.

36 On ecclesiastical imperialism see Angarrack, J. (1999). *Breaking the Chains: Propaganda, Censorship, Deception and the Manipulation of Public Opinion in Cornwall.* Camborne, Cornish Stannary Publications, *passim.*

37 See Bakere, J. A. (1980). *The Cornish Ordinalia; A Critical Study.* Cardiff, University of Wales Press, pp. 93-97.

storyline to make Pilate responsible for Joseph's incarceration, a most unusual variant of the tradition, suggesting perhaps a lost vernacular source. This heightens the drama, but also ties in with the wider theme of legitimate versus illegitimate authority and the abuse of power which is found right across the Cornish language drama, in the plays featuring the tyrant Teudar for instance.[38] The Cornish play, instead of following the racial stereotype of the time and blaming the Jewish people, makes the foreign power guilty of the injustice to Joseph, and this may be a coded reference to English oppression in Cornwall, especially as the victim was so closely identified with tinners and the tin trade. In an extraordinary twentieth century survival of this association, Henry Jenner recalled that

> Some years back in north London during the making of tin sheets for organ pipes, before the molten tin was poured a man said, every time: "Joseph was in the tin trade"[39]

The tinners who filled the seats in the "playing places" must surely have identified with their patron when he appeared on stage.

The imprisonment of Joseph in the play is one of the incidents given a specifically local context by a grant of Cornish land. Pilate rewards the gaoler who takes Joseph away to his "lightless dungeon":

> "Because you are such a trustworthy gaoler, I bestow upon you the manor of Kennall in its entirety, plus Carminow and Merthen as well."[40]

In the play Pilate is motivated by fear that the friends of Christ will stage his "resurrection", that "multitudes will believe him to be none other than the God of Heaven: all Judea will fall into chaos and Rome's authority be swept away".[41]

---

38 See Poscoe, W. H. (1985). *Teudar – A King of Cornwall*. Redruth, Dyllansow Trurau.

39 Quoted in Lewis, *op. cit.*, p.32.

40 All references are to Markham Harris's translation (1969). *The Cornish Ordinalia: A Critical Study*. Washington, Catholic University of America, p. 181.

41 *Ibid.*, p. 179.

Pilate's attitude towards Joseph also serves to emphasize the Roman governor's guilt for the death of Christ, which medieval Christians often laid upon the Jews, as Joseph's friend Nicodemus says:

> "What a crime you have committed sir! Such an end for such a man was so grievous a sight it very nearly struck us blind."[42]

Of course, the playwright's main concern is to tell the story of Christ's Passion and atonement for sin, not to provide an allegorical account of Cornwall's colonial predicament, but he also wanted to tell his story in a way that made sense to an audience composed of his own people, and in achieving his artistic purpose he may have told us more about them than he himself was aware of.

The imprisonment scene is followed by Christ's harrowing of Hell, also from the Gospel of Nicodemus: Adam and Eve and the other redeemed souls are led away to Paradise by the Holy Spirit. The emancipation of these prisoners parallels the release of Joseph and Nicodemus by the angel Gabriel. Further scenes portraying the responses of the disciples to Christ's resurrection are followed by the death of Pilate, which some have considered to be an interpolation, partly because of the inconsistency between the sympathetic Pilate of the trial scene and the villainous Pilate of the "Death" scene.[43] In this scene, which has no warrant in scripture, there is a considerable amount of legendary material including Saint Veronica and the miraculous healing of the leprosy from which the Emperor Tiberius suffers. The Emperor condemns Pilate:

> into a merciless death preceded by scathing torments from which no man may shield him.[44]

Like Joseph he is sent to the dungeon "there to rot in total darkness" for the crime of crucifying Christ: the legitimate exercise of (Roman) power is opposed to the local tyrant's abuse of power, in

---

42   *Ibid.*, p. 179.
43   Bakere, *op. cit.*, p. 41.
44   Harris, *op. cit.*, p. 231.

what may be a dim echo of Arthur's fight against the encroaching Saxons. Whether the scene is an interpolation or not, its presence suggests a desire to portray Pilate in a negative light, and an implication that such a treatment would go down well with a Cornish audience. Lines like

> "Take and throw him in the hole. Don't hold back or pay any attention to his noise, as he's of no account. And let's not have any grumbling from you. He's got to go the distance, definitely, and can't sidestep what's coming to him."

have a certain relish to them. And the fact that this scene is not present in the play's known sources is also interesting.

Death and Resurrection

The fourteenth century, when the *Ordinalia* was written, saw the creation of the Duchy of Cornwall, replacing the former earldom. The new duchy, whatever romantic claims may have been made for it since, owed its existence to the British crown and was the personal fiefdom of the heir to the crown.[45] As Bernard Deacon says:

> because of the lack of an heir the duchy was actually in Crown hands for seventy-one of the 120 years from 1377 to 1497. And kings appear to have disposed, disrupted and restored the duchy at will in the late medieval period.[46]

In such circumstances the questions of legitimacy and the abuse of power must have been ever-present in Cornish minds. In 1497 sparked by oppressive taxation and the suppression of the Cornish Stannary Parliament, the "duchy" rose in revolt, led by Michael Angove, the St Keverne blacksmith, and Thomas Flamank, a lawyer from Bodmin. Though this rebellion had specific causes in common with other revolts in Britain at the time, it was clearly grounded in an historic sense of Cornish identity. Though this dream died in the

---

45 See Deacon, B. (2007). *A Concise History of Cornwall*. Cardiff, University of Wales Press, pp. 36 ff.

46 *Ibid.*, p. 37.

bloodbath at Blackheath it is hard to believe that some of the rebels at least did not pursue the vision of another world in which Cornwall might take its rightful place.

Faced with an atrocious death Pilate kills himself in despair. He is buried but the earth rejects his corpse, which turns black. Eventually they put the body in an iron chest and throw it into the Tiber, where it poisons the water. St Veronica advised that the corpse be raised, put in a boat and floated down to the sea, which will transport it to Hell, "with the curse of God, angels and holy men upon him".[47] This is done and the body is taken away by devils, "to a complete assortment of never-ending torments". That is the end of Pilate, and the play concludes with Christ's triumphant Ascension to Heaven, the otherworld which awaits us all, since

> God the Father, through the operation of the Holy Ghost has sent salvation into the world, while above us God the Son shall dwell on high forever.[48]

The Legend of the Rood

Also from the Gospel of Nicodemus the Cornish dramatist borrowed the Legend of the Rood, which he uses to link together the three plays of his trilogy. This dramatization of the Rood legend is unique in Britain, though versions of it survive in French and Low German.

The story begins with Adam, who sends his son Seth to Heaven to seek the Oil of Mercy that will absolve him from his sin of disobedience in eating the apple.[49] Seth is struck by the beauty of the otherworld:

> "God in Heaven, how lovely it is! How great the sorrow of him who lost it!"

He sees the serpent who tempted Eve in the branches of the Tree of Knowledge, and on the highest branch a baby, symbolizing the

---

47   Harris, *op. cit.*, p. 238.

48   *Ibid.*, p. 246.

49   See Halliday, F. E. (1955). *The Legend of the Rood.* London, Duckworth. And Quinn, G. C. (1962). *The Quest of Seth for the Oil of Life.* Chicago, University of Chicago Press.

Christ-child who will save the world from sin, and who is Himself the Oil of Mercy. The angel gives Seth three seeds from the apple which his father stole and tells him to plant the seeds in Adam's mouth after he is dead. This he does (this part of the story seems to derive from some apocryphal Jewish source). The seeds grow into three wands, prefiguring the Holy Trinity of God the Father, Son and Holy Spirit, and are later discovered by Moses who plants them in a secret place before he dies. An angel tells King David where to find the wands which are by now joined into one. David performs various miracles with the shining branch, eventually planting it and building a garden around it. For thirty years the tree flourishes and every year the king nails a silver circle around the trunk to measure its growth. (These eventually become the "thirty pieces of silver" with which Judas is rewarded for betraying Jesus.) When David's son Solomon builds his famous Temple he uses the holy tree to make the master beam, but however it is cut it is never the right length, and eventually it is placed in the Temple and another tree is used for the roof.

One day a lady called Maximilla comes to worship at the Temple and sits on the holy tree, when her clothes catch fire and she begins to prophesy about Jesus' crucifixion. She is accused of blaspheming the gods and beheaded, and her soul rises to Heaven where she is greeted as the first Christian martyr. For a while the beam serves as a bridge over the brook of Siloah and eventually it is used to make the cross on which Christ is crucified. The Cornish play shows us Moses discovering the "three shining rods... as an evidence and a token of the three persons in the Trinity",[50] which is of course an anachronism, like Maximilla's martyrdom: in the Otherworld time is not an historic continuum but an everlasting mythic present. After Moses" death an angel appears and tells David to take the rods home with him to Jerusalem. On the journey the rods bring healing to three men who are blind, lame and deaf.

The building of the Temple by King Solomon is preceded by another land grant, this time from the king to a messenger:

---

50   Harris, *op. cit.*, p.46.

"To you also sirs, my profound thanks. If I live, you will hold top rank in my bodyguard, and because I received the crown at your hands I shall bestow upon you Bosvannah, Lost-withiel and Lanner."[51]

Thus the play is situated in contemporary Cornwall as well as in historic Palestine: in much the same way as Moses can be assured of the Holy Trinity long before the doctrine has been formulated, or Maximilla can be a Christian martyr long before the birth of Christ. In this world truth can transcend the logic of time and space.

In this case the Cornish names are followed by other Cornish references as the second messenger swears "by Saint Gylmyn", an otherwise unknown Cornish saint, and Solomon rewards his masons with a further land grant, "the parish of Rudock, plus Seal Rock with all its land".[52] These parishes were apparently derelict at the time and the gift evokes a sardonic response: "Oh such generosity!" from the second mason. These references, though they convey little today, must often have produced a knowing response from the audience, and helped break down the barriers that separated it from the play, an effect already facilitated by the shape of the theatre, the involvement of local people in the production, and the convivial drinking which concluded each day's drama. Unlike conditions in a modern urban theatre, the audience all knew each other. In a sense they also helped to relocate "salvation history" itself and bring it closer to the community.[53] And though the story of Seth did not originate in Cornwall the play marks it out as being of particular importance there. The story itself tells of a redemptive force working through history to emancipate the human race, a global theme certainly but perhaps also a particularly Cornish one.

The holy tree is the only one suitable to provide the roof beam for the Temple, and Solomon reluctantly agrees to have it cut. But when the carpenters try to saw the beam it always turns out to be too long or too short, however carefully they measure it. Another beam is found and the holy wood is placed in the Temple. Solomon closes

---

51 *Ibid*, p. 65.

52 *Ibid*, p. 67.

53 See Coleman, W. *Plen-an-Gwari: The Playing Places of Cornwall.* Golden Tree Publications.

the episode with another Cornish land grant, and the incident of Maximilla's martyrdom follows, as we have seen. The beam is carried off to make a bridge at Bethsaida and the *Origo Mundi*, the first play in the trilogy, comes to an end.

The next play, *Passio Christi*, opens with Christ himself announcing salvation and proclaiming the otherworld to come, in

> "his kingdom, where there is neither trouble nor strife, but only joy, sure and everlasting in the company of the angels. Heart cannot conceive the bliss that shall be yours through all eternity."[54]

Various incidents follow from the life of Christ leading up to his trial and crucifixion. When Jesus is dead Joseph of Arimathea begs Pilate to let him have the body for burial, offering to bury him in his own sepulchre. In a moving scene Joseph, Nicodemus, and Mary anoint the body of Christ. We hear no more of the Holy Tree, though fragments of it crop up and are venerated all over medieval Europe, all derived from the "true cross" discovered by Helena, the Emperor Constantine's mother, who divided it into four parts, one each for the Temple, Rome, Alexandria and St Sophia in Constantinople, where it continued to work miracles until the city fell to the Turks.[55]

The Land of Promise

Dreams of a better world are always with us. In some circumstances that better world may be identified with a lost golden age, part imaginary and part real, in which a desirable future is identified with past greatness, and contrasted with present misery and insignificance, in a peripheral Cornwall for instance. The "Legend of the Rood" was one way of resisting cultural appropriation by asserting Cornish distinctiveness in the distinctively Cornish setting of the Cornish language drama, while at the same time underpinning Cornwall's traditional links with continental Europe. The tendency of the medieval mind to link stories together seems to have been particularly strong in Cornwall, and through the person of Joseph

54 Harris, *op. cit.*, p. 81.

55 *Ibid.*, p. 173.

of Arimathea, and the story of the Holy Visit Cornwall is also linked to Glastonbury, its own Arthurian tradition, and the European literature of the Grail Quest as well as the "salvation history" told in the Bible. Within this unifying vision categories of time and space dissolve, as they do in the *Ordinalia* and in the folktales in which a day in the Otherworld can be years of our time, just as it can occupy the same space as ours and yet be invisible to us, as in the story of Cherry of Zennor. We remember too characters in Irish and Manx stories who spent years with their fairy lovers though it seemed but a day to them.[56] To enter the otherworld is to renounce the categories that make human life possible. But those who do so often pay with their lives, like poor Anne Jefferies, forever exiled from her fairy lover in a "real" world in which she no longer belongs.[57]

Mermaids too embody this same ambivalence. Though they live in another world they occasionally appear on the borders of ours where the sea meets the land, and are

> ladies seen on the rocks... going off from the shore to peculiar, isolated rocks at special seasons... ladies sitting weeping wailing on the shore.[58]

Inhabitants of the otherworld usually share this liminal quality, like the Irish sidhe who live under the earth but also over the sea in Tír na nÓg where Oisín went with Niamh of the Golden Hair. Bran visited it on his famous voyage, which may also include some real geographical locations.[59] Tír na nÓg is also Tír Tairngire, the Land of Promise, the destination sought by St Brendan on his voyage, associated with Manannán mac Lir, the sea-god after whom the Isle of Man is named. This may be the same place as Tír faoi Thoinn, the Land under Wave, another home of the Tuatha Dé Danann.[60] A closely related theme is that of the submerged city, of which there

---

56 For 'Cherry of Zennor' see Hunt, *op. cit.*, pp. 120-126. See also 'Oisin in the Land of Youth' in Cross. T. P. and Slover, C. H. (eds.) (1936, reprint 1996). *Ancient Irish Tales*. New York, Barnes and Noble, pp. 439-456.

57 Hunt, *op. cit.*, pp. 127-9.

58 *Ibid.*, p. 148.

59 Meyer, K. (1895, reprint 1994). *The Voyage of Bran*. Felinfach, Llanerch.

60 MacKillop, *op. cit.*, p. 388.

are traces in Cornwall, at Langarrow and Tresillern in Trewartha Marsh, and of course the lost land of Lyonesse in Mount's Bay.[61] Other examples from the Celtic lands include Ys in Brittany, Cantrer Gwaelod in Cardigan Bay and Shannon City. How or if these lost cities relate to the undersea home of the mermaids is unclear.

In some respects these otherworlds represent wish fulfilment (eternal feasting and the charms of golden-haired Niamh, for instance), and on a less exalted level we find this in the Cornish folktale too: when Anne Jefferies meets her otherworldly lover, for instance:

> This gentleman looked so sweetly on Anne that she was charmed beyond measure, and she put down her hand as if to shake hands with her little friend, when he jumped into her palm and she lifted him into her hap. He then, without any more ado, clambered upon her bosom and neck and began kissing her. Anne never felt so charmed in her life.[62]

This is heady stuff for "the daughter of a poor labouring man" in St Teath, and it is clear that understandable desires for wealth, status and sex or affection play a role in the genesis of folktales, especially where the dominant culture is perceived as repressive, as Methodism sometimes was. Mermaids too seem to offer possibilities of sexual fulfilment (they seem originally to have lacked the fishtails with which we now invariably picture them) though they are often more vengeful than erotic. At Lemorna there is a "mermaid's rock" to which young men are said to have swum, lured by the mermaid's song, only to be drowned. At Seaton the mermaid legend comes together with the lost city. The story goes that the mermaid was "injured" by local sailors, and her curse caused the city to be buried in sand. Much the same thing happened at Padstow harbour. In some respects mermaids resemble Scottish silkies and other super-natural entities of the western coasts, and it is hard to resist the conclusion that many mermaid stories have been lost. It is clear though that like the otherworldly beings encountered by Cherry of

61 Deane and Shaw, *op. cit.*, pp. 125-6.
62 Hunt, *op. cit.*, p. 128.

Zennor and Anne Jefferies they were dangerous, and relations with them, however desirable, were to be avoided.

The imagined world then redresses the balance of the real: it can, in fantasy at least make up for the limitations of the present which are always with us. Where these limitations are shared they can generate a shared fantasy of a better world, which may also be a restoration of the world as it was, or is thought to have been, before everything went wrong. The redemptive fantasy then is about the reparation of loss. So Arthur the sleeping king will return to redress all wrongs. Dreams of redemption may be dreams of freedom as perhaps they were in the time of Jesus himself, some of whose followers were zealots who wanted to overthrow Roman rule. The confusion between these two different sets of aspiration led to the crucifixion of Christ, as we see from the Cornish Passion play. His revolutionary potential was a threat to the occupying power.

It is this transgressive quality which gives the otherworld its liberating power, because class divisions and injustice will be no more. As Christ says to Dilmas, the Good Thief:

"I say to you truly that before the evening of this day you shall be with me in Paradise, your faith rewarded."[63]

In the more prosaic world of the folk tale, "poor Jenny", Cherry of Zennor and Anne Jefferies find a world of peace, plenty and love, where:

Hill and valley were covered with flowers, strangely varied in colour but combining into a most harmonious whole: so that the region appeared sown with gems which glittered in a light as brilliant as that of the summer sun yet as mild as moonlight. There were rivers clearer than any water she had ever seen on the granite hills, and waterfalls and fountains; while everywhere ladies and gentlemen dressed in green and gold were walking or sporting or reposing on banks of flowers, singing songs or telling stories. Oh it was a beautiful world.[64]

---

63 Harris, *op. cit.*, p. 166.
64 Hunt, *op. cit.*, p. 117.

The imagery here evokes the world of the rich, leisured classes from which poor Cornish servant girls would normally be excluded. The imagined "otherworld" offers an escape which is denied in real life.

At the beginning of this chapter we quoted Blake on Christ's supposed visit to Britain with his mother and Joseph of Arimathea. But Blake's imagined "Jerusalem" was not an attempt to find solace in the hard, new world of "dark satanic mills": it was a call to arms, an attempt to change the world:

> "Bring me my bow of burning gold
> Bring me my arrows of desire.
> Bring me my spear, oh clouds unfold
> Bring me my chariot of fire!
> I shall not cease from mental fight
> Nor shall my sword sleep in my hand
> Till we have built Jerusalem
> In England's green and pleasant land."[65]

---

65   See Damrusch, L. (2015). *Eternity's Sunrise: The Imaginative World of William Blake.* New Haven, Yale University Press.

Chapter 2

Arthur the Cornishman

The Saint and the Knockers

The Middle Cornish play *Bewnans Ke*, "The Life of St Kea", created great excitement when it was discovered in the year 2000, among the papers of Professor J. E. Caerwyn Williams bequeathed to the National Library of Wales.[66] Especially interesting was the long section dealing with King Arthur, the only surviving Cornish text of its kind. Though much of this material deals with Arthur's conflict with Lucius Hiberius, a fictional Roman emperor, and is the stuff of later medieval legend derived from Geoffrey of Monmouth, there are distinct traces of an older Cornish tradition, and of themes of distinct relevance to Cornwall around the middle of the fifteenth century, when this play was probably written. As we have seen, this was a tense period in Cornish history.

Arthur for instance, is driven by the need to preserve British independence by denying the emperor the tribute which he demands:

> "Lavar the'th arluth, cosyn:
> me re leverys heb flows,
> rag an trubut a wovyn
> na goyth nahen war nebas ous
> the'n stat a Rome,
> mars e ben ef dybynnys.
> Mar goyth pan ew govynnys,
> me a'n danfen thy yuys,
> by the dredful day of dom!
> Yea, bys vycken
> nyns a nahen

---

66   See Introduction to Thomas, G. and Williams, V. (2007). *Bewnans Ke: The Life of St. Ke*. Exeter, Exeter University Press.

rag Bretayn Veer
the'th arluth mas." (ll. 2112-24)

"Tell your lord, my friend:
I have said without trifling,
as for the tribute he demands
there does not fall for some time now
to the state of Rome,
anything other than his decapitated head.
Since it is insolently demanded,
I shall send it thither indeed,
by the dreadful day of doom!
Yea, for ever
nothing else will go
from Great Britain
to the goodly lord."[67]

Throughout the king is "Arthur Cornow", Arthur the Cornish-man, "flowra an bys / a Gyllywyk", the flower of the world / from Kelliwyk (Arthur's Cornish base). Rather pointedly for a Cornish audience, a stage direction refers to him as *Arthurus Rex Britannie: que nunc Anglia dicitur*, "Arthur King of Britain, which is now called England").[68] In a curious image Lucius is said to be so powerful that he can even inspire fear in the "goblins under the earth".

"ny vith mab den na'm dowtya
na whath graflost yn dan dor.
Me ew Lucie, an empror..." (ll. 1641-3)

"there will be no man who does not fear me
nor even any goblin under the earth.
I am Lucius the emperor"[69]

While the "Ninth Legate" addresses him thus:

---

67   *Ibid.*, pp. 212-15.
68   *Ibid.*, l. 1396 f.
69   *Ibid.*, p. 168-69.

"Eth os floran
drys peb i'n noer
An vothygan
in dan an doer
a'th worth heb mar (ll. 1765-69)

You are the flower
beyond all men in the earth.
The goblins
under the earth
revere you without doubt."[70]

These comments are part of a string of conventionally hyperbolic praises of Lucius which serve to emphasize both the obsequiousness of the legates and the magnitude of Arthur's achievement in defeating him. They would no doubt have been received ironically by the audience. Though Arthur himself is praised he is not credited with power over "the goblins under the earth". The words translated here as "goblins" are "gravlost" and "bothiak". Thomas and Williams gloss the former as "subterranean goblin or demon" whereas Ken George gives "kravlost", literally "scrape tail" meaning "knocker" (the well-known mine spirit known from Cornish folklore). Though this is perhaps not much to go on it does suggest the longevity of the folk belief in knockers, many of whose stories were recorded by Robert Hunt in the 1840s.

The Cornish knockers were mine-spirits, relatives of the German kobolds but much more friendly. They were supposed to be the spirits of Jewish people who had once worked in the mines as a punishment for their supposed involvement in the crucifixion of Christ. They and their related spirits had many names—buccas, gathorns, knickers, nuggies, and spriggans for instance, and the distinction between these groups is not always clear.[71] Unlike the kobolds they are friendly to the miners, if treated well. Hunt tells the story of Trenwith and his son, who could communicate with the knockers:

70 _Ibid._, p. 181.
71 See Briggs, K. (1976) _A Dictionary of Fairies_. London, Penguin, p. 255.

they told the little miners that they would save them all the trouble of breaking down the ore that they would bring "to grass" for them, one tenth of the richest stuff, and leave it properly dressed, if they would quietly give them up this end (of the mine). An agreement of some kind was come to. The old man and his som took the pitch, and in a short time realised much wealth. The old man never failed to keep his bargain, and leave the tenth of the ore to his friends. He died. The son was avaricious and selfish. He sought to cheat the knockers, but he ruined himself by so doing. The lode failed: nothing answered with him: disappointed, he took to drink, squandering all the money had made, and died a beggar.[72]

As often in folktales generosity and fair-dealing are rewarded, while duplicity and greed are punished, and this of course affirms the values which small communities depend on for survival. Also, in the dangerous life of the miner it was important to avoid the hostility of the natural, and supernatural forces which might endanger life. The claim that the emperor Lucius can command such powers is therefore extremely grandiose. In the event the emperor's attempt to subdue the British and their leader Arthur "the Cornishman" proves as vain as any attempt to subdue the subterranean goblins would do, and his head is sent back to Rome in ironic tribute. The scene in which these metaphors are used follows the one in which Kea confronts the tyrant Teudar, with an intervening scene emphasizing Arthur's greatness, and picks up the same theme, that of unjust foreign rule, a theme which in Cornwall could only be tackled in subtly encoded ways.

The "Real" Arthur

It is necessary to be clear when discussing King Arthur about precisely what and whom we mean. First we must separate the historic personality from his many fictional representations. The historical Arthur is often described, with some justification, as "shadowy". He is first mentioned in Wennices' "Historia Brittonum" as a "dux bellorum" or war leader, who led Celtic resistance to the

72   Hunt, *op. cit.*, pp. 90-1.

invading Saxons defeating them in twelve battles in the late fifth century.[73] Gildas also describes the Saxon invasions, explaining them in terms of moral failings on the British side.

Arthur's twelfth victory at Mount Badon, near Bath, checked the English advance and secured a generation of peace. This much seems to be clear, though there is only one other early reference to Arthur found in the Welsh poem of the *Gododdin*. The *Gododdin* were a British, Celtic people who lived in what is now southern Scotland. At some point in the last decade of the sixth century a band of their warriors rode south to fight the Saxons at "Catraeth", modern Catterick in Yorkshire, where they were slaughtered. The poem, which is of uncertain date, celebrates the courage, loyalty and lifestyle of the Celtic warriors. Though scholarly debate continues about the language of the poem, which can seem obscure, the events it describes certainly took place and were long remembered by the Britons of Strathclyde and north Wales, the "men of the north". They took place before the old British language fragmented into Welsh, Cambrian (which seems to have died out in the ninth century) and Cornish, at a time when Cornwall was part of a British nation which was still fighting fiercely to preserve its independence.

The Arthurian reference occurs in a passage describing the exploits of "Gwawrddur", a hero of the *Gododdin*:

> "He fed black ravens on the rampart of a fortress
> Though he was no Arthur.
> Among the powerful ones in battle,
> In the front rank Gwawrddur was a palisade"[74]

The reference is slight, but it does demonstrate the existence of a British and later Welsh (and perhaps Cornish tradition, though there is no surviving Cornish literature from this date) that Arthur was remembered, and associated with resistance to Anglo-Saxon hegemony. Otherwise the comparison between Arthur and Gwawrddur, who are also associated in the "canur meirch", would hardly make sense.[75] Little is known of Gwawrddur with whom his

73 See Myres, J. (1986). *The English Settlements.* Oxford, Clarenden Press. pp. 8-20.

74 Jarman, A. O. H. 1988). *Aneirin: Y Gododdin.* Llandysul, Gomer Press, p. 65.

75 Bromwich, R. (ed.) (2014, fourth edition). *Trioedd Ynys Frydein: The Triads of the*

name is associated here, except that he was one of the men "who paid for his mead feast with his life".

Though most scholars agree that Arthur's operations were centred in the north, he has long-standing associations with Cornwall. The Welsh annals say that he died at Camlan, possibly the Camel River, from which Camelford is named, or the Kemyel River near Lamorna cove, both in Cornwall, in a final battle with his nephew Modred and his Saxon allies. It is hard to be certain, though the existence of an Arthurian tradition in tenth century Cornwall is evident. The king's identification with Cornwall is substantiated by a strange incident that occurred in Bodmin in 1113. Some French canons from Laon were on a fund-raising visit in that year, and when one of them scoffed at the local belief that Arthur still lived a riot ensued. Obviously local people still felt a strong identification with the king and believed the legend that he had never died and would one day return to save his people.

The legend of the sleeping hero is ancient and widespread.[76] In the middle ages it was particularly associated with Brittany, though Robert of Gloucester says that the Cornish shared it. In 1582 the Spanish writer Julian del Castillo recounted the traditional belief that Arthur had been enchanted into the form of "a crow", a story that recalls that given to Hunt by his informant Edgar McCulloch, whose father was walking along Marazion Green one day with his fowling piece on his shoulder, when:

> he saw a raven at a distance and fired at it. An old man who was near immediately rebuked him, telling that he ought on no account to have shot at a raven, for that King Arthur was still alive in the form of that bird.

Hunt adds that, in his enquiries about Arthur,

Islands of Britain. Cardiff, University of Wales Press, pp. lxxx iii-iv.

76   See Westwood, J. (1985). *Albion: A Guide to Legendary Britain*. London, Granada, pp. 6-9.

Nowhere do I find the raven associated with him, but I have been told that bad luck would follow the man who killed a chough, for Arthur was transformed into one of these birds.[77]

The colour of the bird's red beak and talons was said to mask Arthur's violent death. The modern Cornish poet Nicholas Williams affirms the traditional belief:

> "Nyns yu marow myghtern Arthur
> nyns yu whath yn sur
> rag un jeth y whra dewheles
> dh'agan rewlya-ny gans gwyr…
>
> King Arthur is not dead
> Indeed, he is not dead
> for one day he will return
> to rule us with justice…"[78]

The motif of the sleeping hero who will return at the time of his people's greatest need (A580) is often connected with other motifs such as hidden treasure or the sleeping army,[79] as in the legend of Alderley in Cheshire, brilliantly exploited by Alan Garner in his 1960 children's book *The Weirdstone of Brisingamen*. The story seems to have originated in the eighteenth century and in the earliest versions the sleeping king is not named, but the Victorians identified him as Arthur. In a letter of 1838 Mrs Gaskell wrote to a friend:

> If you were on Alderley Edge, the hill between Cheshire and Derbyshire, I could point out to you the very entrance to the cave where Arthur and his knights lie sleeping in their golden armour till the day when England's peril shall summon them to her rescue.[80]

---

77 Hunt, *op. cit.*, pp. 308-9.

78 Berresford-Ellis, P. (1974). *The Cornish Language and its Literature*. London, Routledge and Keegan Paul, p. 189.

79 See Thompson, C. (1977). *The Folktale*. Berkeley, University of California Press, pp. 262-4.

80 Westwood, J. and Simpson, T. (2005). *The Lore of the Land*. London, Penguin,

It is interesting to note that already Arthur has been appropriated by the dominant culture as an English king, and it is of course extremely unlikely that any authentic Arthurian tradition could have survived in Cheshire, a county in which such associations are almost unknown. A similar story was told at Sewingshields in Northumberland whose sleeping king is also identified as Arthur, and at a few other northern sites, which has been used as evidence of a northern location for the conflict of Camlann, Arthur's last battle, which other scholars site in Cornwall.

As we have seen, Hunt commented on the scarcity of Arthurian traditions in Cornwall, which surprised him. A visit of 1803 turned up no stories in either Tintagel or Camelford, though of course absence of evidence is not evidence of absence. He does tell the story of "The Battle of Vellan-Driechar" in which Arthur defeats a huge army of invading Danes whose fleet is destroyed by a magical storm.[81] Arthur and his allies drink the water of St Sennen's Well. It is interesting that the few Arthurian stories that survive, though they are probably late, do depict him as a fighter against foreign oppression: even if they are inventions they clearly reflect a popular feeling that this is the kind of thing Arthur would have done.

The Cornish site with which Arthur is more associated is of course Tintagel. In fact, though Geoffrey of Monmouth does name Tintagel as the seat of Gorlois, Duke of Cornwall, the place where Arthur was conceived, this is the stuff of medieval romance rather than Dark Age history. Tintagel Castle is a medieval ruin. The fact that the Anglo-Norman earls of Cornwall based their authority there may, as Philip Payton suggests, have been an attempt to exploit its Arthurian associations, derived from Geoffrey of Monmouth, to bolster their own legitimacy.[82] But it might also have worked the other way. The very real power of the earls, based at Tintagel, could have encouraged the belief that Arthur had once ruled there, especially in later centuries when memories of the earls themselves grew vague. In either case of course the association of Arthur with legitimate political authority in Cornwall is presumed. The medieval ruins correspond to the Arthur of medieval romance who lives on

pp. 74-5.

81   Hunt, *op. cit.*, p. 305.

82   Payton, P. (2004). *Cornwall: A History*. Fowey, Cornwall Editions, pp. 58-59.

into our own time, the Arthur of chivalry, knights in armour and the Round Table, and these are the associations which modern visitors bring to the site. This is another act of cultural appropriation, reinforced by the film industry: as the stage directions in *Bewnans Ke* reminds us, Arthur is *Rex Brittanie, qui nunc Anglia, dicitur*; "king of Britain which is now called England". So far as Tintagel is concerned it is in any case unlikely that the notion of an administrative capital can have meant much to a peripatetic war-band leader to whom mobility must have been a key asset.[83]

The Legend

If the historic Arthur lived in the sixth century, the legendary Arthur was born in the twelfth, with Geoffrey of Monmouth as midwife. In or around the year 1138, Geoffrey wrote his famous *History of the Kings of Britain* based, he claimed on "a most ancient book in the British tongue".[84] Such a book has never been found, though Geoffrey may well have had access to Welsh sources which have since been lost, as well as the works of Nennius and Bede which he certainly made use of. Though his reliability has been questioned ever since his own day his contribution to the Arthurian legend is undoubted. His book was translated into many languages, most importantly French, and the stories became a staple of courtly romantic literature, a genre which transcended national boundaries and became the basis on a new European sensibility. Geoffrey tells the story of Uther Pendragon's seduction of Ygaerne, the wife of Gorlois of Cornwall, with the aid of Merlin's magic, as a result of which Arthur is conceived. Arthur becomes king of Britain at the age of fifteen and embarks upon a series of conquests. He holds court at Caerleon, the City of the Legions and marries a Roman lady called Guanhomara, later famous as Guinevere. The Emperor Lucius demands tribute from him but he refuses and this is the background to the Arthurian scenes in the "Life of St Kea". Arthur's defiance in Geoffrey's account must have made a strong appeal to the Cornish dramatist:

83   For a more positive view of Tintagel's Arthurian links see Seddon, R (1990). *The Mystery of Arthur at Tintagel*. London, Rudolf Steiner Press.

84   See Introduction to Lewis, T (ed.) (1966). *Geoffrey of Monmouth: The History of the Kings of Britain*. Harmonasworth, Penguin.

When these men landed with their armed band and conquered our fatherland by force and violence at a time when it was weakened by civil dissentions, they had been encouraged to come here by the disunity of our ancestors. Seeing that they seized the country in this way, it was wrong of them to exact tribute from it. Nothing that is acquired by force and violence can ever be held legally by anyone.[85]

And this of course was the situation in which Cornwall found itself.

The Arthur of Romance

Most of the Arthurian romances which followed derived ultimately from Geoffrey's *Historia*, and they are too many to mention here. In the twelfth century the Norman writer Wace based his *Roman de Brut* on Geoffrey, added "the Round Table" motif and referred to the British belief that Arthur would come again. Layamon's *Brut*, based on Wace, was the first English version of the story, and it shows Arthur being carried off after his last battle in a magic boat, to the Isle of Avalon. The story was further developed by great writers such as Chrétien de Troyes, Marie de France, and others, and became the core of a body of tales which became known as the "Matere of Britain".[86] Other characters such as Tristan, Lancelot and Merlin were added to the mix, and Arthur's court became the starting point from which other heroes set off on their knightly adventures, as in the middle English masterpiece, *Sir Gawayne and the Green Knight* for instance. The fullest expression of the Arthurian legend in English is Sir Thomas Malory's *Morte d'Arthur*, derived from "a French book", which places great emphasis on the quest for the Holy Grail, and the loves of Tristan and Iseult, Lancelot and Guinevere.[87]

These motifs of course fitted well and indeed helped to create the conventions of what came to be called "amour courtois" or courtly love, first developed by the Provencal troubadours in the twelfth century. In this paradigm love became an ennobling almost spiritual passion. Such love was passionate, premarital or extramarital, and

85   *Ibid.*, p. 232.
86   See Chretien de Troyes (1975). *Arthurian Romances*. London, Dent. And Busby, K. (ed.) (1986). *The Lais of Marie de France*. London, Penguin.
87   See Vinaver's excellent edition in 'Malory: Works', second edition (1971).

was always perhaps more of an ideal than a social reality, which is just as well since its conclusion was frequently tragic, and its literary highpoints were de Lorris and de Meun's *Roman de La Rose* and Dante's celebrated "Vita Nuova", in which the poet celebrates his idealized love for Beatrice.[88] The emotional world evoked here is radically different from the Celtic tales of triadic love in which individuals are trapped in a web of conflicting loyalties from which they cannot escape: one thinks of the stories of Lleu Llaw Gyffes, Blodeuwedd and Gronw Bebyr in the *Mabinogion*, and in Ireland Derdriu and the sons of Usneach and Diarmuid and Gráinne, a group of stories to which a Cornish "original" of Tristan and Iseult, if it ever existed, must certainly have belonged.[89] In the literature of romance Arthur is generally an important part of the story's framework, but as the triadic relationship with Lancelot and Guinevere develops he becomes a tragic participant. In this sense the story returns to what may have been its original form, the queen's adultery and the destructive conflict with Medrout.

It is generally impossible to discern the precise outline of "original" stories beneath medieval romance or even to define what "original" might mean in stories that are, in all probability, as old as human history. Nor is the movement of stories necessarily linear, i.e. from Celtic original towards a sophisticated French narrative and then onwards to a Hollywood movie or a computer game. We have seen that authentic Arthurian tradition persisted in Cornwall, yet the writer of *Bewnans Ke* borrowed his account of the Roman war from Geoffrey of Monmouth to create a play for Cornish audiences in his own time. The belief in the sleeping king existed in Cornwall (though not in Cheshire) long before Geoffrey wrote and seems to have persisted for centuries afterwards. The central role of Breton storytelling in diffusing Arthurian legend has long been recognized:

> Scraps of evidence here and there demonstrate that the
> Bretons, or people familiar with Breton versions of Arthurian

---

88 See Drabble, M. (2006, Revised 6th edition). *The Oxford Companion to English Literature*. Oxford, Oxford University Press, p. 258.

89 See Jones, G. and Jones, T. (1949, reprint 1970). *The Mabinogion*. London, Dent. And Cross, T. P. and Slover, C. K. (eds.) (1936. reprint 1996). *Ancient Irish Tales*. New York, Barnes and Noble, pp. 239-247; pp. 370-421.

tales, roamed Europe telling of the adventures of Arthur and meeting receptive audiences in many lands. These tellers of tales we know as Breton "conteurs"[90]

As we shall see cultural links between Brittany, Cornwall and Wales were strong throughout the Middle Ages until the marginalization of the Celtic lands imposed by the growing English and French nation-states at the time of the Reformation, and the Bretons were ideally placed to translate the old, oral tradition into the sophisticated literary culture of medieval France, which came to dominate Europe. But the process may have been reflexive, as motifs from Arthurian romance found their way back to Cornwall, for instance, their original home; in the *Mabinogion*, especially in the later stories, we see the tone and style of the French romances applied to ancient Welsh traditions.[91]

A manuscript does at least provide a basis for discussion about sources and mutual influences, even if interpretation can be difficult, but the precise interactions between oral traditions and literatures in many different languages may never be known. The question is further complicated by the fact that oral tradition in Cornwall was fading just as the French literary tradition was growing in strength and influence. That Cornish tradition played an important part in the genesis of European romance literature through Breton intermediaries who must have inherited some of that tradition, is clear, though the extent and precise nature of that influence will never be clearly known, nor the extent to which that literature fed back to Cornwall and Brittany to influence the tradition itself.

Every writer who has made use of the Arthurian legend has done something to it, and the Middle Ages liked to join stories up into a coherent whole, though to us the joints might seem rather arbitrary at times. One result of this was to create a vast web of associations linking one story with another, and this was a particular tendency of Cornish culture, even in its fragmented state. So in the story of Joseph of Arimathea in the apocryphal Gospel of Nicodemus which was popularized in Europe by Robert Le Boron's poem written late

---

90   Eisner, S. (1969). *The Tristan Legend: A Study in Sources*. Evanston, Northwestern University Press, p. 14.
91   See Jones and Jones, *op. cit.*

in the twelfth century. In this version Joseph was a secret Christian employed as a soldier by Pontius Pilate, who collected the blood of Christ in a cup which had been used at the Last Supper, the famous "Holy Grail".[92] He then gave the Grail to his assistant Bron, with instructions to take it to the west, and William of Malmesbury expanded this into a legend that Joseph visited Britain and founded the first Christian church there.[93] In this version Joseph was descended from King David, and in the thirteenth century prose romances he becomes the ancestor of Galahad and Lancelot, the Knights of the Round Table. Another knight, Perceval was a relative of Peleur, the "fisher king" and guardian of the Grail, who was himself descended from Joseph: Tristran, Gawain, and even Arthur himself are also said to be descended from Joseph in other versions of the story.

So Joseph of Arimathea formed a link between the Arthurian legend and the still greater narrative of Christ's death and resurrection, as well as countless lesser stories. The Cornish story of the Holy Visit linked him and his stories to the Cornish landscape and the historical experience of the Cornish people, and his presence in the medieval Cornish drama emphasizes his centrality in this nexus of stories. Through him it connected with the "big narratives" of Christianity and European literature, and making its own contribution through Tristan and Arthur. It is tempting to see this as a cultural strategy, a response to the "older peripheralization imposed on Cornwall by the English nation state",[94] though the Cornish legend is not recorded until Sabine Baring-Gould's *Book of Cornwall* in 1899.[95]

"Courtly love" was about the cultivation of a particular kind of sensibility, a sensibility that never had much social reality. Arthur's devotion to Guinevere, Tristan's doomed love for Iseult, were rarely seen in real lives, and adulterous relationships were frowned on by the Church and condemned by society generally. The older Celtic stories, of which traces survive in *Tristan* were neither romantic nor

---

92   See Bromwich, R., *op. cit.*, pp.405-6.

93   See Treharne, R. F. (1967). *The Glastonbury Legends*. London, Sphere Books.

94   See Payton, P. (1992). *The Making of Modern Cornwall*. Redruth, Dyllansow Trurau, Chapter One.

95   Baring-Gould, S. (1899). *A Book of Cornwall*. London, Methuen.

moralistic, but inherently tragic, moved with a kind of heroic pessimism which still carries conviction and emotional force.

Arthur and the British Project

Stories of course are told to serve a purpose, and sometimes unconscious or contradictory purposes of which even the storyteller may be unaware. The stories of Joseph of Arimathea at Glastonbury and the discovery of Arthur's body there were obviously helpful in strengthening the status and legitimacy of the Abbey, though that in itself does not make them untrue on other levels. The stories people tell help define who they are but such stories can also be manipulated by others to serve their own purposes as the Tudors appropriated the story of Arthur to bolster their own credibility, which in fact was based on the slaughter at Bosworth and not much else. If English rule in Cornwall was felt to be illegitimate that might explain why it was so important to the Cornish dramatists, though the importance of the issue extended far beyond the fifteenth century and far beyond Cornwall: Shakespeare of course explores it in his cycle of history plays. At around the time *Bewnans Ke* was staged, Henry VII was trying to co-opt the Cornish gentry into what Philip Payton calls his "British Project", using the mechanism of the Duchy of Cornwall to reward his loyal supporters: he even named the new Duke of Cornwall "Arthur". But his suspension of the rights of Cornwall's ancient "Stannary Parliament" in 1496 lost him much support among working-class Cornish people, and it has been claimed that tinners provided most of the footsoldiers in the rebellion of the following year. Arthur thus became both the personification of Cornish nationhood and the symbol of the Tudors' new nation state, and "Arthur the Cornishman" began his long career in the service of "the British Project", within which Cornwall and its people were progressively marginalized and disempowered, though the sense of identity and connection with Arthur did persist, as *Bewnans Ke* proves.

Historians from A. L. Rowse to Mark Stoyle have emphasized the Cornish aspirations that lay behind the risings of 1497, 1549, and 1642 though these events also involved people from outside Cornwall and issues which were not specific to Cornwall. But by the seventeenth century memories of violent conflict between Briton and

Saxon were fading, and spurious reconciliations were engineered. In Wales for instance James I, like Henry VII was claimed as a descendant of Arthur by the ruling dynasty, legitimizing his rule. But old beliefs were not far below the surface, and they were to erupt in the English Civil War. In Cornwall the split between the common people and the gentry, which had been bought off by the Crown, grew wider, and towards the end of the fifteenth century English replaced Cornish as the majority language.[96] In Cornwall moreover, religious innovation imposed by the English Reformation further alienated local people who saw the old religion as more sympathetic to their language and culture: on the English side this reinforced anti-Catholic paranoia, which helps to explain, though it cannot excuse, the ferocity with which the "Prayer Book Rebellion" was suppressed.

In the Civil War Cornwall came out for the king and by the summer of 1643 the "Cornish army" controlled Devon. It was soon superceded by Sir Richard Grenville's "New Cornish" troops, and at one point Sir Richard proposed a separate peace with Parliament guaranteeing Cornwall's independence as an autonomous royalist statelet under his own control. For a while Grenville's troops made Cornish separatism a reality by sealing off the Tamar

> as well from the rebels as from such unruly (royalist) troopers
> as doe plunder and abuse the country

but in the end nothing came of the plan, which remains one of the great "might have beens" of Cornish history.[97] Parliamentary victory put an end to Cornish hopes, though England had not heard the last of the Cornish and their king.

Purcell's King Arthur

King Arthur, or The British Worthy, a Dramatic Opera, the text by John Dryden, with music by Henry Purcell, was produced in May 1691 at the Queen's Theatre, Dorset Gardens. According to a contem-

---

96 Stoyle, M. (2002). *West Britons: Cornish Identities and the Early Modern British State.* Exeter, University of Exeter Press, p. 20.

97 Stoyle, M. (2005). *Soldiers and Strangers: An Ethnic History of the English Civil War.* New Haven, Yale University Press, pp. 186-8.

porary account "it pleased the court and city, and being well performed, was very gainful to the company". In fact, the work is a "semi-opera", a combination of drama, poetry, music, dance and elaborate scenic architecture, a hybrid born of French court ballet and the native Jonsonian masque tradition rather than as opera in the modern sense, of which the only contemporary examples were John Blow's *Venus and Adonis* and Purcell's own *Dido and Aeneas*.[98] Purcell composed some of his finest music for these "semi-operas" which include *The Fairy-Queen* and *The Indian Queen*. They are all characterized by:

> the great importance of the chorus, and abundance of instrumental numbers (ritanelli, dances, precluded and descriptive pieces), spoken dialogue, very few recitatives (all of the arioso type), elaborate sets and stage machinery, and the fact that none of the principal characters sing.[99]

Dryden wrote the text as "the last piece of service which I had the honour to do for my gracious master King Charles the Second", although Charles was dead by the time it reached performance, and William III was leading the Grand Alliance against the French in the Netherlands. In 1685 Dryden had collaborated with the French composer Graby to produce *Albion and Albanius*, a work which prefigured "King Arthur" in its thematic concerns, but which proved a flop with the theatre-going public. Blow and Purcell did not conceal their opinion of the Frenchman's awful score and this seems to have provoked a certain coldness on Dryden's part: by 1691 however he was prepared to acknowledge that:

> Music has since arrived to a greater perfection in England than ever formerly, especially passing through the artful hands of Mr Purcell, who has composed it with so great a genius that he has nothing to fear but an ignorant, ill-judging audience.

---

98 See Harman, A. and Milner, A. (1983). *Late Renaissance and Baroque Music*. London, Barrie and Jenkins.

99 *Ibid.*

These words display both generosity and sound judgement, though elsewhere in his Preface he does complain that

> The numbers of poetry and vocal musick are sometimes so contrary that in many places I have been obliged to cramp my verses and make then ragged to the reader, that they may be harmonious to the hearer."

One wonders whether Dryden was uneasily aware of the contrast between Purcell's delightful score and his own rather pedestrian libretto.

The plot of the piece has a chaotic fatuity which makes it difficult to describe. It opens at the point when Arthur, "having won ten victories", has recaptured most of his kingdom from Oswald, the Saxon king, who is also his rival for the favours of Emmeline, the Duke of Cornwall's blind daughter. Ormond, Oswald's court magician, employs two spirits, Grimbald and Philidel, to support the Saxon cause, but Merlin persuades Philidel to go over to the British side; he also restores Emmeline's sight. Osmond is also attracted to the beautiful Cornish heiress and betrays Oswald. He further attempts to trap Arthur who instead captures Grimbald who has been disguised, for reasons into which we need not inquire, as Emmeline. In Act V Osmond and Oswald patch up their differences and the latter fights a duel with Arthur, which of course he loses. Arthur with characteristic magnanimity releases Oswald and restores him to Emmeline. There is a storm followed by a tableau depicting Britannia rising from the azure main, and in conclusion a fulsome eulogy of Britain, her people and her monarch, characteristically blurring the question of Arthur's "Britishness" and identifying it with seventeenth-century England. It is this spurious unity which is being celebrated: they create a desert and they call it peace.

But what one remembers most about "King Arthur" is Purcell's glorious music: the "Frost Scene with its strange harmonies and remarkable tremolandos, the seemingly endless succession of fine ensembles and solos, and the virtuoso display of Act V, which includes the songs, "Ye Blustering Brethren", "For Folded Flocks" and particularly "Fairest Isle", in which Albion is the recipient of hyperbolic praise:

> "Fairest Isle, of all isles excelling,
> seat of pleasure and of love:
> Venus here will choose her dwelling,
> and forsake her Cyprian Grove."[100]

And it is this song which brings us closest to the underlying political and social purposes of the piece. By the 1690s the Arthurian legend was in the doldrums and there were two principal reasons for this.[101] Post Reformation England had come to associate the once and future king with a medieval Catholic past, a past which the new Protestant middle-class was anxious to forget. Moreover, the astute use of the legend by the Tudors which reached its finest flowering in Spenser's allegorical poem *The Faerie Queen* rendered it too royalist for the rising bourgeoisie, particularly of course during the commonwealth. Charles I was executed in 1649, and the murder of God's anointed was accompanied by a wave of hooliganism directed against the remnants of popery, as we can still see in countless vandalized parish churches, and the suppression of music and the licentiousness of the theatre. Even after the Restoration the fictitious "Popish plot" of 1678 uncovered a depth of anti-Catholic prejudice anticipating the Islamophobia of more recent times, and it was James II's pro-Catholic sympathies which provoked the so-called "Glorious Revolution" which swept William of Orange to the throne.

It is this background which allows us to understand the first performance of "King Arthur". England in 1691 had endured two major constitutional changes and a vicious civil war within living memory. The king was engaged in a continental conflict the consequences of which could not be foreseen: while at home two generations of conflict had shaped a nation ill at ease with itself. In

100 Mathews, J. and Stewart, R. J. (1995). *Merlin Through the Ages*. London, Blandford. This anthology contains the text of 'Merlin, or The British Enchanter' which is the title given to Dryden's 'King Arthur in its Later, Eighteenth-Century Performances'. The text is printed in its entirety, except for the Prologue and Epilogue, from the Clerll edition of 1726.
101 Knight, S. (1983). *Arthurian Literature and Society*. London, MacMillan.

Dryden's Libretto we find a sentimental affirmation of personal relationships a world away from the "real" Arthur's life and death struggle for survival, but a natural response to the uncertainties of the time, perhaps:

> "Cupid from his favrite nation
> Care and envy will remove,
> Jealousie that poysons passion
> And Despair that does for Love."

along with appeals for unity:

> "Britons and Saxons shall be once one people;
> One common Tongue, one common Faith shall bind
> Our jarring Bounds, in a perpetual Peace."

and affirmation of national greatness:

> "Retire and let Britannia Rise
> In Triumph o'er the Main.
> Serene and calm, and void of fear,
> The Queen of Islands must appear."

The fragility of the Arcadian imagery which studs Dryden's verse betrays a deep ambivalence. Hope that the Williamite settlement will heal England's social and psychological wounds is undermined by fear that it will not, and the fantasy is tinged by desperation. The solution suggested here is a spurious unity based on coercion, not mutual tolerance and respect: "One common tongue, one common faith", that is, Protestantism and the English language. The fate of Cornwall and the Cornish language is already clear, though Arthur's role in the "British Project" is not yet over.

One Common Tongue

Towards the end of the seventeenth century the last Cornish monoglots passed away, and though the Bosons and a few others attempted to create a new literature this was no more than a small scale academic exercise. The ensuing century did see the beginnings of serious study of the Cornish language when Edward Lhuyd, the keeper of the Ashmolean, visited Cornwall. Lhuyd published a Cornish-English vocabulary and was the first scholar to divide the Celtic languages into "Q" Celtic (Irish, Manx, and Scottish Gaelic which retained the original "Q" sound as "c"), and the "P" Celtic or Brythonic group, comprising Welsh, Breton, and Cornish. A great opportunity was lost when Jesus College passed up the chance of buying Lhuyd's manuscripts on his death. Antiquarians such as Borlase and Price might have gathered more fragments of Cornish than they did had they not been hampered by prejudice against "those who had no Latin". Meanwhile the last speakers died. Dolly Pentreath, generally credited as being the last speaker of traditional Cornish, died in 1777. Though she was almost certainly not the last speaker, it is clear that:

> With her death one of the few remaining repositories of the language vanished without anyone noting down one word of her knowledge.[102]

Individuals such as John Nancarrow of Marazion, Jane Cock, and Jane Woodcock of Mousehole were known to be able to converse in Cornish after Mrs Pentreath's death, and revivalists have also cited prayers and other fragments as evidence that the language never died, and although it is true that:

> a language does not die suddenly, snuffed out with one last remaining speaker.[103]

still it must be said that as a social medium Cornish was effectively dead by the end of the eighteenth century, and so passed the most potent symbol of Cornish identity.

It was replaced by a new industrial identity. After a brief period of ultra-royalism, religious dissent set down firm roots in Cornwall and among the common people Methodism flourished to an extent unique in southern England (a similar process took place in South

---

102 See Beresford-Ellis, *op. cit.*, Chapter 5.
103 *Ibid.*, p. 123.

Wales). At the same time the Duchy became increasingly incorporated into England as just another county. The growing involvement
of capital investors in the tin industry undermined the traditional
partnerships between working miners but increased output and the
overall size of the industry, while the expansion of tin-plate
manufacture in South Wales created a new demand for Cornish tin.
These years also saw the beginnings of the china clay industry which
was to play an important role in the Cornish economy.[104] The
Cornish people though paid a high price for entering the world
market. Poverty and industrial accidents took a high toll of human
life and emigration waxed and waned to the rhythm of boom and
bust: there were even grain shortages and the mining communities
were driven to take "undue measures" to lower the price. In 1812
for instance this report appeared in the "West Briton":

> On Monday last the miners who reside between Redruth
> and Truro, assembled in great numbers and proceeded to
> the houses of several farmers, whom they induced to sign a
> written agreement to sell them wheat at 30 shillings, and
> barley at 15 shillings a Cornish bushel, of three Winchester
> bushels. When this engagement was signed and corn
> delivered in compliance with it, the miners offered no
> violence, but contented themselves with soliciting bread, an
> article of food which some of them declared they had not
> tasted for several days.[105]

Many men faced the choice of working in the growing mining
industries of Australia, South Africa and California or staying at
home to starve. The rate of spousal separation was high, disrupting
family life and creating a remittance culture in the mining communities of the west. Though little survives in the way of personal
records, the burden on women must have been heavy.[106] And

104 See Rowe, J. (1993). *Cornwall in the Age of the Industrial Revolution*. St. Austell,
      Cornish Hillside Publications, Chapter 2.
105 Barton, R. M. (1997). *Life in Cornwall in the Early Nineteenth Century*. Redruth,
      Truran, pp. 27-8.
106 Trotter, L. (2012). 'Husband Abroad' *Cornish Studies 20* (2012) (ed. Payton, P.),
      pp. 180-99.

meanwhile the appropriation of Cornish labour and raw materials, and the appropriation of Cornwall itself as an English county, were paralleled by the appropriation of Arthur as an English king.

Imperial Arthur

As we have seen, Henry VII laid the groundwork for this by enlisting the legendary king in his "British Project". Henry VIII later had Arthur's "round table" (actually a thirteenth-century fake) repainted in the Tudor colours and moved to Winchester. Spenser's *Faerie Queen*, written in the 1590s portrays "Prince Arthur" as an example of the perfect unifying ruler, identified with Elizabeth, England's own "Gloriana", and King James was similarly glorified in Arthurian form, in Ben Jonson's masque "The Speeches at Prince Henry's Barriers".[107] But Victorian Britain had different needs. The monarchy was now well-established as a brand, but the new business class required heroes more in keeping with its status as the world's dominant industrial and colonial power. In the nineteenth century the Middle Ages were a lost world in which the religious and class divisions of a perplexing and conflicted present had not existed. The newly imagined Arthur also embodied the chivalric ethical code which they aspired to and which they needed to justify their claims to power and status. The fact that the historic king was a British resistance leader was deliberately blurred, and it remains so. Arthur had indeed returned, in the shape of the Duke of Wellington (Arthur Wellesley), to unite his people and lead them to victory against the French.

In a world of profound social and economic dislocation medievalism, phoney as it was, helped provide a sense of continuity, and Arthur had an important role to play in that: he was a chivalric ideal for the Victorians but also a source of reassurance in troubled times, when even the existence of God could not be taken for granted. In Cornwall itself storytelling continued to bind communities together though the loss of the language combined with large-scale emigration and industrialization reduced the Arthurian legend to a trickle. Although Hunt's story about the chough (already old in his time)

107 See Barczewski, S. (2000). *Myth and National Identity in Nineteenth-Century Britain: The Legends of King Arthur and Robin Hood.* Oxford, Oxford University Press, pp. 17-18.

does suggest that the belief in the sleeping king still lingered in odd corners, there is not much else,[108] and what there is, is either literary in origin or frankly spurious, such as the tourist circus at Tintagel, or the suggestion that the famous Excalibur was thrown into Dozmary Pool, an idea probably derived from Tennyson.

Of course Tennyson's masterpiece *The Idylls of the King* was the greatest nineteenth-century contribution to Arthurian literature. This series of poems was published in fragments over many years, and the complete sequence was not published until 1891, though he began writing it in the 1850s. The poems exude a characteristically late Victorian sense of sadness and gloom, as the poet shows Guinevere's affair with Lancelot shattering the unity of the Round Table. Especially in "The Passing of Arthur" section the poet is also expressing his personal sense of loss following the death of his friend Arthur Hallam, unforgettably expressed also in "In Memoriam". His own grief was identified with the sense of loss which permeated a whole society, and both were embodied in the fictional Arthur. Tennyson's Arthur symbolized both the anxieties and the ideals of Victorian England which, while proud of its achievements, was uneasy about what it had become. The legend soothed those anxieties by creating a false sense of unchanging values in a changing world, the image of a man who did his duty in spite of the duplicity of women and foreigners, a man who was "British" in the nineteenth-century sense, through and through. It also provides a sense of adventure in an England which was in reality becoming increasingly tame and suburban and a surrogate spirituality in an increasingly secular world: moral choice and faith are simple in the Arthurian story, the white knight always defeats the black, every young woman is a princess, a "stunner" out of a Waterhouse painting, and conflicts between desire and loyalty are resolved, unless they survive as fragments of a Celtic original. Such fantasies are now a significant component of popular culture, and though often dismissed as "escapist", they help us to survive in an increasingly dystopian world, though they also hinder us from changing it. The Arthurian legend still performs these functions, though in a degraded

---

108 On a recent visit to Glastonbury I expressed doubt about the authenticity of Arthur's grave there. The young female guide told me that many visitors expressed similar doubts, adding "they say that King Arthur never died".

commercialized form, and it has had a strong influence on the fantasy genre through "Sword and Sorcery" films, gaming and the like.[109]

Arthur and the Revival

To the modern world of course Arthur no longer represents chivalry, Christian ideals or national unity. When the National Lottery was introduced in Britain in the 1990s, the lottery machines were called Guinevere, Lancelot and Arthur; in the computer game *Legion: The Legend of Excalibur*, you can take the role of Arthur yourself and have adventures with your friends Merlin and "Gwen".[110] Arthurian war gaming is popular, and Arthur also has a role in New Age spirituality.[111] The legend has permeated late capitalist culture at a time when that culture itself is fragmenting.

On a much smaller scale Cornwall also recreated an Arthur of its own, and although much of this activity was designed to serve the interests of the tourist industry, some of it constituted a serious attempt to incorporate the tradition into a contemporary movement for emancipation. The appropriation of Arthur that we have seen, though it was never led by reputable scholars, did encounter some scholarly resistance in Cornwall. Henry Jenner is best known as the founder of the Cornish language revival: he published his famous *Handbook of the Cornish Language* in 1904. Though Jenner himself seems to have believed that a Cornish-speaking Cornwall was no longer possible or desirable, his book was an important affirmation of Cornish cultural identity. It may be doubted whether anyone has ever learned to actually speak Cornish from Jenner's *Handbook* but it did spark a genuine revival and enable others, such as Robert Morton Nance and A. S. D. Smith to build on his foundations: what Jenner did was to unashamedly present the language as a mark of identity:

---

109 See Mersey, D. (2004). *Arthur King of the Britons: From Celtic Hero to Cinema Icon.* Chichester, Summersdale, Chapter Six. I bought my copy of this book in Poundland, which illustrates the breadth of Arthur's appeal.

110 *Ibid.*

111 See Hutton, R. (2008). *Witches. Druids and King Arthur.* London, Bloomsbury.

Why should Cornishmen learn Cornish? There is no money in it, it serves no practical purpose and the literature is scanty and of no great originality or value. The question is a fair one, the answer is simple. Because they are Cornishmen. At the present day Cornwall, but for a few survivals of Duchy jurisdictions, is legally and practically a county of England, with a county council, a county police and a Lord-Lieutenant all complete, as if it were no better than a mere Essex or Herts. But every Cornishman knows well enough, proud as he may be of belonging to the British Empire that he is no more an Englishman than a Caithness man is, that he has as much right to a separate patriotism to his little motherland, which rightly understood is no bar, but rather an advantage to the greater British patriotism, as has a Scotsman an Irishman, a Welshman, or even a colonial...[112]

This though carefully phrased, is a call for a radical realignment of the relationship between Cornwall and "the great enlightened nation", a new paradigm which allowed space for Cornish identity. It is also of course ambivalent about that identity, and this ambivalence is still present in contemporary Cornwall, an inevitable consequence of its history. But Jenner's radicalism should not be underestimated here. For the first time the language is being promulgated not as an antiquarian exercise, as it was for the Bosons for instance, but as an enactment of shared identity.[113] Nor did Jenner back away from the consequences of his position. In 1904, the same year in which his *Handbook* was published, he made an impassioned speech entitled "Cornwall, a Celtic Nation", to the Pan-Celtic Congress at Caernarfon, and Cornwall was admitted to membership of the Congress.[114] Cornwall had discovered its lost voice in more ways than one.

112 See Preface to Jenner, H. (1904). *A Handbook of the Cornish Language*. London, David Nutt. New edition, *Henry Jenner's Handbook of the Cornish Language*, edited by Michael Everson, Cathair na Mart, Evertype, 2010.

113 See Williams, D. R. (2004). *Henry and Katheerine Jenner*. London, Francis Routle.

114 The speech is reprinted in Jenner, H (1996). *King Arthur in Cornwall*.Penzance, Oakmagic.

In that paper Jenner makes a powerful case for Cornwall's Celtic past, based on the language and its relationship to other Celtic languages. He declared his belief in Cornishness and its future grounded not in the enthusiasm of middle-class zealots, but in the common people, "An Werin" in Cornish:

> They are of all classes in the community, no doubt, but certainly a very large proportion belong, not to the rich and leisured class, who might take up Cornish as a fashion, as they take up golf or motoring but to the classes of hard-working clerks, small business man, shopkeepers and artisans, the classes that form the backbone of Cornish Methodism—a very different sort of people from the same classes in a non-Celtic country.[115]

Like most revolutions this was a return to the past, and although Jenner did not pursue the political implications, others did.

Though the Arthurian legend was not exactly central to Jenner's Cornish project, he did make some attempt to reclaim it for Cornwall. In 1911 he wrote two papers on Arthurian themes. The first, dealing with possible Arthurian place-names in West Penwith, was read at the summer meeting of the Royal Institution of Cornwall. The second, "Tintagel Castle in History and Romance" was read at Tintagel itself on 22 June 1926, as the castle was actually being excavated.[116] Archaeologically there is little to link Tintagel with the Arthurian period, let alone Arthur himself, as Jenner makes clear, and the claims of Castle Dore are stronger.[117]

In "Some Possible Arthurian Place-Names" Jenner brings all his considerable linguistic erudition to bear on the map of West Penwith, and produces some interesting hypotheses linking a number of sites with the names of characters in the Arthurian cycle. He does not make exaggerated claims for these links, and the etymology is rarely conclusive, as in the case of "Bosworlac", a farm in St Just said to be named after Gorlois, the husband of Igerna. There are at least two

---

115 *Ibid.*

116 Reprinted in Jenner (1996).

117 See Hencken, H. O. (1932). *The Archaeology of Cornwall and Scilly.* London, Methuen and Co.

major problems here: firstly, which medieval text can we regard as closest to a hypothetical British/Cornish original, and secondly, even when the etymology is right, how can we be sure that the person commemorated is the character in the story, and not someone else who happened to have the same or a similar name? The name "Modred", for instance, occurs in contexts (in inscriptions and deeds for instance), which suggest that it was a common name in Cornwall, perhaps for some centuries, which makes it impossible to say that it refers to Arthur's nephew. So far as it goes, this supports the hints in Welsh tradition that Mordred was originally a popular figure, but such questions will never now be answered.

What Jenner did was nonetheless important. By making an imaginative connection between the landscape and the legend he repatriated the story and returned it to its proper owners, not in any deceptive or grandiose way but by using story to give meaning to the landscape in which the people of Cornwall still live, much as the *Ordinalia* writer did with his Cornish place-names. The stories which the community tell itself affirm its identity and its place in history. That Arthur's is also a global story affirms Cornwall's place in the wider world, as the *Ordinalia* did.

Jenner's second paper was on "Tintagel Castle in History and Romance". For many Tintagel is the centre of Cornwall's Arthurian story. This, like much else in the story, goes back to Geoffrey of Monmouth who tells of Uther Pendragon's desire for Igerna, the beautiful wife of Gorlois, Duke of Cornwall. Merlin disguises Uther in the form of Gorlois; Uther then sleeps with Igerna, and Arthur is conceived. The story with all its dramatic potential resurfaced in later medieval romance and became an important part of the legend, forever linked with Tintagel, and the ruined castle there. Unfortunately Tintagel Castle was built in 1140, over six hundred years after Arthur's time, and although there is some evidence of sub-Roman activity on the site, there is no clear link with the historic Arthur.[118] The story of Uther, Gorlois and Igerna is nonetheless interesting and in some respects out of place in medieval romance. It is closer to the theme of triadic love and conflict prominent in

118 See Ralegh Radford (1968 reprint 1979). 'Romance and Reality in Cornwall'. In Ashe, G. (ed.) (1979). *The Quest for Arthur's Britain*. London, Paladin, pp. 59-72.

Celtic literature for instance in the stories of Blodeuwedd and Derdriu (see Introduction), in which the conflict between desire and loyalty leads to violence and social disruption. In the Tintagel story Uther and Gorlois fight a war over Guinevere, and the legend goes on to describe the war between Arthur and Modred which leads to Camlann, fatally weakening the British cause. A similar pattern is to be found in Béroul's *Tristan and Iseult*, though there it has a thick, romantic overlay. Béroul's story also takes place in a distinctively Cornish landscape.

Celtic Roots

The other strikingly Celtic theme in the story of Arthur's conception is that of shapeshifting: Merlin transforms Uther into the likeness of Gorlois in order to enjoy his wife: shapeshifting or metamorphosis occurs in different mythological traditions around the world. The euhemerized gods of early Irish literature often changed shape, or died and were reborn. The great Irish hero Cú Chulainn for instance seems to have been a reincarnation of the god Lugh, and Mongán was also conceived magically and by deceit by the sea-god Manannán Mac Lir with the queen Caintigern: Mongán was said to be a reincarnation of the great hero Fionn mac Cumhaill. In the haunting story of "The Wooing of Etain", the heroine, who was perhaps originally a sun goddess, is reborn as the daughter of Etar, king of Ulster. Midir created fifty women who resembled her exactly.[119]

Various mythological characters possess the ability to assume different forms, some of them representing the impersonal forces of nature; Amergin, the first Irish poet, declared:

> I am the wind that blows over the sea
> I am the wave of the ocean: ...
> I am a wild boar in valour,
> I am a salmon in the water....
> I am the god that creates in the head of man the fire of thought.
> Who is it that enlightens the assembly upon the mountain if
>   not I?

119 See McKillop, *op. cit.*, *passim*. And retellings in Cross and Slover, *op. cit.*

Who telleth the ages of the moon if not I?
Who showeth the place where the sun goes to rest if not I?[120]

The Welsh poet Taliesin too has a curiously protean personality and a mysterious origin:

> Primary chief bard am I to Elphin,
> And my original country is the region of the summer stars.
> Idno and Heinin called me Merddin.
> At length every being will call me Taliesin...
> I have been with my Lord in the ass's manger,
> I strengthened Moses through the waters of Jordan:
> I have been in the firmament with Mary Magdalen
> I have obtained the muse from the cauldron of Ceridwen
> I shall be until the day of doom on the face of the earth
> ... and it is not known whether my body is flesh or fish.
> Then was I for nine months
> In the womb of the witch Ceridwen:
> I was originally little Gwion
> And at length I am Taliesin.[121]

These strange verses also recall the story of Tuan mac Cairill in the Book of the Dun Cow. Tuan was the oldest man in Ireland and had been there from the beginning, undergoing several transformations as an eagle, wild bear and so on. Whether these stories echo some ancient belief in the transmigration of souls which Caesar famously reported among the Druids is uncertain. In literary terms it allows individual characters to reappear in different contexts, and to link different narratives together.

Though no poetry of this kind survives in the Cornish language, the debate on the dual nature of Christ in the *Ordinalia* is an interesting parallel. In the *Passio Christi* two scholars debate Christ's claim to be both God and man, itself a kind of reincarnation. One scholar asserts the contradictory nature of such a claim, "for God

120 Rolleston, T. W. (1911). *Myths and Legends of the Celtic Race*. London, Harrap, p. 134.
121 *Ibid.*, pp. 416-17.

and man are two things very contradictory in nature", but the other says

> "ef a alse bos yn ta
> hanter den ha hanter dev
> den yv hanter morvoron
> benen a'n pen the'n colon
> yn della yw an ihesu." (ll. 1740-44)

> "He might be well
> Half man and half God
> Human is half the mermaid,
> Woman from the head to the heart;
> So is the Jesus."[122]

The transformation of God into man is even more radical than the transformations of Taliesin and Tuan mac Carrell. But in Cornish culture too we find the same concern for connectedness and intertextuality, as the Arthur legend illustrates a connectedness which embraces both sacred history and wider historical contexts, even though the culture itself is fragmented. The Arthurian legend itself reflects such concerns.

Henry Jenner however, reached the rather melancholic conclusion that:

> Altogether, Tintagel Castle, considering how famous it is, especially in modern imitations of Arthurian romances, has singularly little history and not much romance attached to it, when one comes to sum it up, and it was probably not really the scene of the one incident that brought it into notice. Historically and romantically Tintagel Castle is a bit of a fraud.[123]

Yet in our own mass culture, which is also fragmented in what we have come to call a characteristically post-modern way, Arthur

---

122 Norris, E. (1859). *The Ancient Cornish Drama*. Oxford, Oxford University Press, vol. I, pp. 360-61. See also my own *Gathering the Fragments* (2016), pp.14-15.
123 Jenner, *op. cit.*, p. 36.

retains an important place, even if it is in the service of commercial values. In fact the Arthurian legend has been used to serve different agendas, from Gildas to the present, and mostly it has been pressed to serve the interests of power, as we have seen. In Cornwall, though, and perhaps elsewhere it may still retain something of its emancipatory power and point towards another world in which Cornwall is not an alienated colony but a free country with a proud culture of its own. The Cornish language revivalists of the early twentieth century turned naturally to Arthur to embody their hopes and dreams. In his short 1932 play, *An Balores* "The Chough", Robert Morton Nance uses the chough as a metaphor for the language, and the play opens with the stage direction:

> An bobel, peswar den ha dyw venen, a sef adro un vasken vyghan, warnedhy palores varow, yn-dan elerlen.

> The people, four men and two women, stand around a little bier, with a dead chough on it, under a pall.[124]

A character in the play, Peter Grief, blames the people of Cornwall for the chough's death:

> Ny, an dus Kernow, yu, re-s-ladhas! Hy res ombrederas, "pandr'a dal dhem bewa, ynnof ow-quytha yn-few spyrys myghtern Arthur, aban na-vyn tus Kernow kewsel Kernewek na-moy?—pandr'a dal bos Arthur bew, marow mar pe y davas?"

> We the people of Cornwall, it is, who have killed it! It thought within itself "What good is it for me to live, keeping the spirit of King Arthur alive in me, since the folk of Cornwall won't speak Cornish any more? What is the use of Arthur being alive if his tongue is dead?"[125]

---

124 Thomas, P. W. and Williams, D. P. (eds.) (2007). *Setting Cornwall on its Feet: Robert Morton Nance 1873-1950*. London, Francis Routle, 128 ff.
125 *Ibid.*, p. 129.

Of course this is polemical, and it does simplify the language issue, but it also enlists the Cornish king on the side of the language revival, and in the end the chough comes back to life. King Arthur and the chough was to be a major theme in the revival.

In the dramatic ritual devised for the Gorseth ceremony and probably written by Nance, the Deputy Grand Bard declares:

"An als whath Arthur a with.
Yn corf Palores yn few:
Y wlas whath Arthur a bew,
Myghtern a ve hag a vyth
An vyrth oll: Nyns yu marow myghtern Arthur!"

"Still Arthur watches our shore
In guise of a chough there flown:
His kingdom he keeps his own
Once king, to be king once more.
All the Bards: King Arthur is not dead!"[126]

English historiography going back to Bede and drawing heavily on Gildas, who had his own fish to fry, had consistently portrayed the original British as a people whose sinful weakness had placed them outside of divine Providence, so justifying the Saxon invasions as divine punishment and placing the Anglo Saxons in direct succession to the Romans as legitimate rulers of the whole of Britain. The Cornish re-appropriation of Arthur was part of a wider attempt to rebut that argument.[127] The underlying racist attitude though persisted long after the historical truth had been forgotten or marginalized, because the whole argument for the legitimacy of English rule in Cornwall depended on it, and it was eventually subsumed into the wider racism that maintained the British Empire. It can still be found in popular culture, as any episode of "Doc Martin" will demonstrate.

The story of the king who rises from the dead inevitably recalls the resurrection of Christ and the other events recorded in the Cornish *Ordinalia* trilogy, as the symbolism of the Irish Easter Rising

126 *Ibid.*, p. 131
127 See Higham, J. (2002). *King Arthur: Myth-Making and History*. London Routledge.

deliberately recalled the same events, to identify the suffering of the Irish people with that of Christ, in order that they might share in His resurrection, bizarre as this might seem to a secularized contemporary world. What has happened in Cornwall is not of course genocide, though some have called it so, but it is "ethnocide", that is:

"a process by which others are forced to transform themselves to the point of fatal identification, if possible, with the model proposed to or imposed on them."

What Jenner, Nance, and their successors today have attempted is the enormous task of attempting to reverse this process.[128] To do that they have used stories.

128 Megaw and Megaw (1997). 'Do the Ancient Celts Still Exist? An Essay on Identity and Contextuality.' In *Studia Celtica* 31, pp. 107-28.

Chapter 3

Tristan and Iseult

The Celtic Context

The story of Tristan and Iseult, whose names are spelled differently in different versions, is one of the most popular and enduring tales associated with the Arthurian legend, into which it was only incorporated at a late stage. Though the story itself is much older, it was taken up by medieval romancers such as Béroul and Gottfried von Strassburg, capitalizing on the popularity of the Arthurian stories and was retold in the beautiful English of Sir Thomas Malory.[129] It has particularly strong links with Cornwall, and with the wider body of ancient Celtic literature with which it has major themes in common. Different versions have different emphases, but the core of the story is this:

Tristan is a prince of Lyonesse, the legendary country now sunk beneath the waves off the west Cornish coast. His mother dies after she has given birth to him, hence his name, which means "sad", and he is brought up at the court of his uncle, King Mark of Cornwall. As a young hero Tristan kills the Irish giant Marholt, who is the brother of Queen Iseult of Ireland. Later the king sends Tristan as an ambassador to Ireland to fetch back the princess Iseult who is to marry the ageing Cornish king. Her mother gives Iseult a love potion to drink on her wedding night, but the two young people drink it on their voyage back to Cornwall, and they then make love. Their relationship continues in secret after Iseult marries the king and is nearly brought to light by Tristan's enemies on several occasions, until eventually the situation becomes intolerable, and Tristan flees the Cornish court.

---

129 See Ferrick, A. S. (trans.) (1970). *The Romance of Tristan by Beroul*. London, Penguin. Von Strassburg, G. (1960). *Tristan*. London, Penguin. Malory, T. (1996). *Le Morte D'Arthur*. Ware, Wordswepth.

While in Brittany he meets another princess Iseult "of the White Hands", and marries her, though his love for the Irish Iseult is undiminished. When Tristan is injured in an affray he sends a message to Iseult Queen of Cornwall to come and heal him. He instructs his servant that a white sail should be raised on his return journey if the queen is with him, and a black sail if she is not. Iseult of the White Hands, Tristan's Breton bride, overhears the conversation and lies to him when the ship comes into sight, telling him that the sail is black. Tristan, thinking his love has deserted him, kills himself and when the queen enters and discovers his body, she dies in despair.

The story enjoyed great popularity in the Middle Ages all over Europe. Its first treatment in modern times seems to have been Mathew Arnold's poem "Tristram and Iseult". From the 1850s on Tennyson's famous *Idylls of the King* raised the profile of Arthurian stories, and helped transform Arthur from a Celtic resistance leader into an English king and this process parallels the transformation of Cornwall into an English county. Wagner's romantic opera *Tristan and Isolde* (1965) brought the story into prominence as well as changing it, but Tristan's story was not wildly popular in late Victorian England. perhaps because of the adulterous theme and the fact that Iseult makes her own sexual choices. In a society which expected a woman to be "the Angel in the house" this could have been quite disturbing, though the story of Arthur, Guinevere and her lover Lancelot is an exact parallel.

Diarmuid and Gráinne

It is perhaps pointless to look for a single origin for a story of which so many versions exist in so many languages, and which in any case reflects so fundamental a human dilemma. The story has parallels in other Celtic languages which are undoubtedly ancient, such as *The Pursuit of Diarmuid and Gráinne*, the greatest narrative in the Irish Fenian cycle, a series of stories about the legendary Fionn mac Cumhail and his war-band, the Fianna. In this story the ageing hero sends messengers to ask for the hand of Gráinne, daughter of the king of Ireland. His request is successful but at the betrothal feast Gráinne falls for Diarmuid, gives everyone else a sleeping potion, and urges him to run away with her, which he does. The lovers run away to the forest, and are pursued by Fionn all over Ireland and Scotland, where their stopping places are still remembered in many place-names.[130] There are many adventures, but Fionn fails to capture the lovers, partly because his followers take Diarmuid's side. (In the Tristan story the dynamics are rather different: three of Mark's nobles hate Tristan and lay traps for him, but they are usually characterized as villains.) Diarmuid joins in with his old comrades in a boar hunt, in which he is seriously injured.

Fionn gloats over the body of the wounded hero, while Diarmuid reminds him that a drink of water from his hands has the power to restore life to the dying, and speaks of all his own brave deeds in Fionn's service. At first Fionn refuses to give him a drink; then, under pressure from his companions he relents, and

> After that Fionn went towards the well, and he took the fill of his two palms with him, and he had not reached more than half way when he let the water run down through his palms, and he said that he could not bring the water with him.[131]

This ending (and there are others) captures perfectly the ambivalence which the main characters share, an ambivalence which seems to have fascinated early audiences. It must be remembered that Diarmuid and Fionn, as Diarmuid says, are bound together by shared experiences and the powerful loyalties which bound a man to his lord and were cemented in combat. Though Fionn is unforgiving we must remember that he is deeply hurt by Diarmuid's disloyalty and the damage to his status and self-esteem caused by the loss of Gráinne, and no-one asks Gráinne if she wants to marry Fionn in the first place. These considerations apply equally to the Tristan/Iseult/Mark triad. All these characters suffer in their different ways and are in different ways trapped in a situation they can do little to alter. Many of these texts have reached us through the hands of monastic copyists, which can give them a misogynistic tone: modern readers may be more in tune with a young woman's

---

130 See Ní Shéaghdha, *op. cit.*, Introduction.
131 *Ibid.*, p.95.

attempts to take control of her own life and more aware of the homoerotic underpinning of war-band culture.

The idea that the Diarmuid/Gráinne/Fionn story was the original of *Tristan and Iseult* was put forward by Gertrude Schoepperle in 1913.[132] James Carney believed that these stories, and the tale of Derdriu and "the sons of Uisnech", a "foretale" of the epic *Táin Bó Cuailnge*, and one of the "Three Sorrows of Storytelling" derived from the late Roman love triangle involving Mars, Venus and her lover Adonis.[133] Whether this is so, and it would be hard to test the links in the chain from pagan Rome to eighth-century Ireland, there is no doubt that the triadic tale of love and loyalty had a special appeal to Celtic audiences over many centuries. A Welsh parallel is found in the *Mabinogion* in the story of Lleu Llaw Gyffes, Blodeuwedd and Gronw Bebyr (in these stories too spellings differ). In this version, Blodeuwedd, a woman made of flowers to be Lleu's wife, plots with her lover Gronw, to kill her husband, for which she is punished by being transformed into an owl.

A Cornish Story

But to what extent can Tristan and Iseult be said to be a Cornish variant of this interceltic story? In the first place it must be said that in the case of such an ancient and protean story there can be no definitive "original". The tale originates in the human heart, in the way human beings are, and expresses truths which resonate across different cultures and times. It might be more helpful to ask if, as part of this chain of stories, a Cornish version might once have existed before the medieval writers turned it into a classic of courtly love? It has long been believed that stories from the Arthurian cycle were brought to France by Breton storytellers, and most scholars agree that the French versions were all based on a British prototype, written in the language from which Cornish later developed, either a text or an oral tradition.[134] That this hypothetical prototype was

132 Schoepperle (1913 reprint 1959). *Tristan and Isolt: The Sources of the Romance.* London and Frankfurt.

133 Carney, J. (1955). *Stories in Irish Literature and History.* Dublin, Dublin Institute for Advanced Studies.

134 See Eisner, S. (1969). *The Tristan Legend: A Study in Sources.* Evanston, Northwestern University Press, Chapter 2.

set in Cornwall seems probable, judging by the accurate Cornish topography of Béroul's *Tristan*, which was written around the year 1170.[135] King Mark was formerly linked to Tintagel, though Béroul places him in "Lancien" (Lantyan), and it is now thought that the historic Mark held court at nearby Castle Dore, an ancient earthwork on the road from Fowey to Lostwithiel. Near this site stands the famous "Tristan Stone", a sixth-century monument bearing the inscription:

> Drustanus hic iacit cunomori filius
> Here lies Tristan, son of Cunomorus[136]

Cunomorus, "Hound of the Sea", or "Great Hound", was another name for King Mark, according to the Latin life of St Paul Aurelian, who met the Cornish king, "Quem alio nomine Quonomoricum", 'who is also known by the name of Conomor'. He is described as:

> a powerful monarch under whose rule lived people of four different languages.[137]

This connection between *Tristan* and King Mark, in the words of Professor Thomas:

> must take Dumnonia's one great legacy to medieval European letters, the romance of Tristan, back to the ninth century and firmly within a Cornish context.[138]

The historic Mark Cunomorus was an effective ruler and diplomat who conquered Dumnonia, the old Celtic kingdom of the southwest, and also controlled territory in Brittany. He was an important

---

135 See Padel, O. J. (1981). *The Cornish Background of the Tristan Stories*. Cambridge Medieval Celtic Studies, *1*, pp. 53-81.

136 Thomas, C. (1994). *And Shall These Mute Stones Speak? Post Roman Inscriptions in Western Britain*. Cardiff, University of Wales Press, pp. 279-80.

137 Doble, G. H. (1941 reprint 1997). *The Saints of Cornwall I: Saints of the Land's End District*. Felinfach Llanerch Press, p. 18.

138 Thomas, *op. cit.*, p. 280.

player in continental politics and died fighting the Frisians in the year 560.[139]

It is noteworthy that the stone describes "Drustanus" (if this is the correct reading) as "son" of Cunomorus, since the legend describes him as the king's nephew. If the stone is right then the story may have been changed to make the relationship between Tristan and Iseult less obviously incestuous. The sixteenth century writer John Leland recorded a line on the stone which has since disappeared:

"Cum domina Clusilla,
i.e. with a lady called Clusilla"[140]

in which "Clusilla could be a version of "Iseult". In fact, there are good reasons for associating all three protagonists in the *Tristan* story with the area around Fowey at what seems to be the right time. The fact that "Drustanus" sounds like a Pictish name—there is a "Drust" mentioned in the Pictish genealogies—has troubled some scholars, but there can be little doubt that the man commemorated on the "Tristan Stone" was the son of the king of Cornwall. Of course this is not to say that he, Iseult and Cunomorus were "the same" as the literary characters created by Béroul, but it certainly supports the contention that at some stage in its long existence the story was set in Cornwall and perhaps also that a written version of it in British or early Cornish did once exist. Like Geoffrey of Monmouth's "Old British book" it is most unlikely to turn up now. It is interesting how many key texts are missing when we come to consider Cornish history and culture. Despite its obvious popularity and many folk-loristic elements, it seems not to have survived in the oral tradition.

The power of the story to hold audiences from Dark Age Cornwall to the present surely lies more in the underlying narrative than in the particular talents of its individual narrators, great as these have sometimes been.[141] Such a history raises fascinating questions about continuity and change and about the relationship between text and

139 Morris, J. (1973). *The Age of Arthur: A History of the British Isles from 350 to 650 A. D.* London, Weidenfeld and Nicholson.

140 Deane, T. and Shaw, T. (2003). *Folklore of Cornwall.* Stroud, Tempus, pp. 128–9.

141 See Ridley Scott's romantic "Tristan and Isolde". Starring James Franco and Sophia Miles: "Before Romeo and Juliet there was Tristan and Isolde".

tradition, questions which will never now be answered. What was the story, "doing" in the six hundred years between the death of the "real" Tristan and its rediscovery by the troubadours? Did it originate in the oral tradition and if so where, since there are few traces of it in that tradition? Of course, aristocratic love stories do not usually make popular folklore. Marie de France in her late twelfth-century "lai", "Chevrefoil" says that her original source is Tristram himself:

> Tristram, a skilful harpist, in order to record his words, as the queen had said he should, used them to create a new lay... I have told you the truth, of the lay I have related here.[142]

This is of course a literary device, though it may be one which Marie herself picked up from the Breton contours. She herself was the first woman of her times to have written successfully in the vernacular, though her own identity is something of a mystery. Her work was part of the burgeoning literature in French which dominated European culture at the time, and she wrote for a sophisticated, aristocratic elite. She used the Tristan story to share the narrative of romantic and adulterous love which was popular in those circles. We still perhaps read the story in similar terms.

A House Divided

But it is unlikely that earlier versions of the story did carry the same romantic implications, or that their audiences placed romantic love above all other considerations, as we are prone to do, at least in theory. *The Pursuit of Diarmuid and Gráinne* for instance, shows an acute awareness of the potentially divisive effects of passionate love within a war-band society, and the twelfth century audience would have been aware of the similar consequences of Lancelot's affair with Guinevere. Chrétien de Troyes, a contemporary of Marie de France tells the story of Lancelot and the Queen, in a version in which love conquers all, though in a lightly ironic style which tends to subvert

---

142 Burgess, G. S. and Busby, K. (eds.) (1984). *The Lais of Marie de France*. London, Penguin, p.110.

the theme. In his introduction to the Everyman edition D. A. B. Owen asks:

> In "Lancelot" is love even held to ridicule and shown to make a wise man foolish?.. Did Chrétien intend us to connive with him, as in some shared joke?[143]

But this is writing of great elegance and sophistication, a world away from the homicidal rivalries of Iron Age warriors which reflect those of the unconscious mind in all ages, rivalries that could and did destroy whole peoples.

Geoffrey of Monmouth wrote his *History of the Kings of Britain*, said to be based on "an ancient British book" early in the twelfth century. Though liberally mixed with legend and fantasy, it is a serious attempt:

> to trace the history of the Britons through a long sweep of nineteen hundred years, from the mythical Brutus... whom he supposed to have given his name to the island after he had landed there in the twelfth century before Christ, down to his last British King Cadwallader who, harassed by plague, famine and dissention and never-ending invasion from the continent, finally abandoned Britain to the Saxons in the seventh century of our era.[144]

Geoffrey does not mention either Lancelot or Tristan, but is well aware of the link between personal relations and social collapse. In his narrative Queen Guinevere is seduced by Mordred, the king's nephew, while the king himself is on the Continent fighting the Romans.[145] Mordred's attempt to seize the kingdom fatally divides the British, and although resistance continued the writing was on the wall for the Celts of Britain.

143 Owen, A. A. R. (ed.) (1975). *Chretien de Troyes: Arthurian Romances*. London, J. M. Dent, pp. xv-xvi.

144 Geoffrey of Monmouth (ed. Lewis Thorpe). *Op. cit.* Introduction.

145 This entirely counter-historical campaign also features in the saints' play 'Bewnans Ke'. In fact Arthur represented the vestiges of Roman authority in Britain.

For seventy-nine years they (the British) harassed the English people with their savage attacks, but little good did it do them. Indeed, the plague about which I have told you, the famine and their own inveterate habit of civil discord had caused this proud people to degenerate so much that they were no longer able to keep their foes at bay. As the foreign element around them became more and more powerful, they were given the name of Welsh instead of Britons.[146]

Mordred and Arthur met in battle at Camlann in Cornwall. Mordred died and Arthur was taken to the Isle of Avallon, which is the old Celtic name for Glastonbury, where he sleeps until his people shall need him again. Just upstream from Camelford, the possible site of the battle was a flat inscribed stone, once thought to mark Arthur's grave, though the Cornish never accepted his death. The inscription is now thought to read:

"Latini hic iacit filius Magari

(The monument) of Latinus. Here he lies, son of Magarus"

which has no Arthurian connection.[147] There is also a grave of Arthur at Glastonbury, containing the relics which were discovered there in 1190 conveniently for the status of the Abbey.

Women were often blamed for the disastrous consequences of adulterous affairs, and Guinevere has certainly had a bad press. As the story developed this may have been because of medieval misogyny, but originally it may have been because in war-band society women were traditionally seen as "peaceweavers", with a crucial role in conflict resolution, and the strengthening of group cohesion. In the warband, such as those led by Fionn and Arthur:

Oath swearing with structured communal drinking was indispensable since it imitated the intimate household pattern: it created a fictive family. And so a mother of the family was also needed—a woman at the core of the group

146 Geoffrey, p. 284.

147 Westwood, J. (1985). *Albion: A Guide to Legendary Britain*. London, Paladin, p. 35.

who might hearten, reward and calm the young men, many of whom, as the institution took root and flourished, were no more than boys seeking training and status...[148]

This relationship had to be idealized in order to reduce the likelihood of sexual attraction, and to strengthen the incest taboo, and so reduce the chance of murderous rivalry. For a woman to step out of this role and become the cause of conflict herself would be unthinkable because it would set up a conflict between the lord and one of his men, and it would of course be considered her fault.

Though it is difficult to uncover beneath the layers of artistic embellishment, perhaps there are traces of this earlier role in Béroul's story of Iseult, in her appeal to her father to spare Tristan's life for instance:

> "Promise that you will pardon this man all his past deeds, no matter what they were, for here he stands to prove that he and no other slew the dragon, and grant him forgiveness and your peace."[149]

and later when Tristan appeals to her to make his peace with Mark:

> "Queen, often and in vain have I summoned you: never since the king drove me away have you deigned to come at my call. Take pity: the king hates me and I know not why. Perhaps you know the cause and can charm his anger for whom can he trust if not you, chaste queen and courteous Iseult?"[150]

But this is designed to deceive the king, who is listening, and no reconciliation with the king, who loves them both, is possible unless they break their relationship. In the romantic narrative love between man and woman takes priority over loyalty and group solidarity.

---

148 Enright, M. (1996). *Lady with a Mead Cup: Ritual, Prophecy and Lordship in the European Warrack*. Dublin, Four Courts Press, p. 283.

149 Bédier, J. (1973) (trans. H. Belloc). *The Romance of Tristan and Iseult*. New York, Random House, p. 283.

150 *Ibid.*, p. 64.

The truth of the Celtic stories is that feelings are often in conflict, and there is no happy ending, and there is always a price to be paid. This tension explains the power of the stories, even though the social context has completely changed, and had completely changed by the twelfth century.

This triad owes much of its power to the fact that it is rooted in the feelings which accompany the child/mother/father triad. Freud described this as the Oedipus complex, though he himself cast doubt upon the objectivity of the theory:

> Freud's actual discovery of the Oedipus complex was made during his self-analysis, though the ground had long been prepared by the analysis of his patients—when he was brought to recognise the love for his mother, which was in himself, alongside a jealousy of his father which conflicted with affection in which he held him; on 15th October 1897 he wrote to Fliess that "we can understand the riveting power of "Oedipus Rex"... the Greek legend seizes on a compulsion which everyone recognizes because he feels its existence within himself... Every new arrival on this planet is faced with the task of mastering the Oedipus complex.[151]

This of course is a circular argument, and the universality of the Oedipus complex is untestable, the evidence for it in non-western cultures slight. There is also a tendency for clinicians to fit clinical material into their own theoretical framework, and non-Freudian therapists do not report Oedipus: we all tend to find what we are looking for, Nonetheless there can be little doubt that the powerful feelings of love and rivalry that underlie these relationships have an important part to play in human development, and that they are often explored in world literature.

Culhwch and Olwen

Another story exploring this theme is the tale of Culhwch and Olwen, found in association with the Welsh *Mabinogion*. Here is a brief summary:

---

151 Laplanche, J. and Pontalis, J. B. (1973). *The Language of Psychoanalysis*. London, Hogarth Press, pp. 282-7.

Cibydd took to wife a woman named Goleuddydd. She became pregnant and went mad, subsequently giving birth in a pig-run to a son who was named Culhwch, after which she died. Cibydd killed a neighbouring king in battle, then married his widow. As Culhwch grew to manhood, his stepmother prophesied that he would never find a wife unless it be Olwen, daughter of the giant Yspaddaden: the boy's father advised him to seek the help of his cousin King Arthur, which he did. Culhwch then set out with Arthur's men for the giant's castle where he met Olwen. She fell in love with him and he with her, unsurprisingly, since:

> She came, with a robe of flame-red silk about her, and around the maiden's neck a torque of red gold, and precious pearls thereon and rubies, yellower was her head than the flowers of the broom, whiter was her flesh than the foam of the wave, whiter were her palms and her fingers than the shoots of the marsh trefoil from amidst the fine gravel of a welling spring. Neither the eye of the mewed hawk nor the eye of the thrice-mewed falcon, not an eye was there fairer than hers. Whiter were her breast than the breast of the white swan, redder were her cheeks than the reddest foxgloves. Whoso beheld her would be filled with love of her. Four white trefoils sprang up behind her wherever she went, and for that reason was she called Olwen (White Track).[152]

Here the object of desire is an old man's daughter rather than his wife, but the rivalry is no less intense, and the giant Yspaddaden is determined to hang on to Olwen. Culhwch asks the girl to elope with him but she has given her word never to leave home without her father's permission, since he is doomed to die whenever she takes a husband, an interesting Freudian proposition. She advises Culhwch to ask her father for her hand in marriage nonetheless, and to perform whatever tasks the giant demands in exchange, a common folkloric motif, and this he does. The giant sets a number of apparently impossible tasks, which Culhwch of course accomplishes,

---

152 Jones, G. and Jones, T., *op. cit.*, p. 111.

with the help of his friends. Then the company returns to Yspaddaden's court:

> And then Culhwch set forth, and Gorell son of Custennin with him, and everyone that wished ill to Yspaddaden Chief Giant came to shave his beard, flesh and skin, to the bone, and his two ears outright and Culhwch said: "Hast thou thy shave man?" "I have," said he, "And is thy daughter mine now?" "Thine," said he, "And thou needst not thank me for that, but thank Arthur who has secured her for thee. Of my own free will thou shouldst never have had her. And it is high time to take away my life." And then Gorell son of Custennin caught him by the hair of his head and dragged him behind him to the mound and cut off his head and set him on the stake. And he took possession of his fort and his dominions and that night Culhwch slept with Olwen and she was his only wife as long as he lived.[153]

This Welsh story recalls Robert Hunt's Cornish droll about "Tom" who killed a giant and took his castle and wife for his own, though the tone is quite different, and the giant's last words are less dignified, if more generous than Yspaddaden's:

> The giant groaned and said: "it's all no good: I shall kick the bucket. I feel myself going round land; but with my last breath I"ll do thee good because I like thee better than anybody I ever met with.[154]

and he leaves his land and possessions to Tom. Superficially both these stories seem very different to the courtly romance of Tristan and Iseult, but the underlying dynamic is the same and it is this that gives them their power and endurance. Young people need to pair up, and developmentally the obstacle to this is the attachment between father and daughter. Symbolically the father must be murdered or must relinquish his daughter to the young man, as the Cornish giant does his wife, so that life can move on. In the Welsh

---

153 *Ibid.*, p. 136.
154 Hunt, *op. cit.*, p. 59.

story, the difficulty is the father's unwillingness to relinquish his daughter rather than the other way round: though all these stories take place in a predominantly male milieu (Hunt heard his story from "a miner on the floors of Ding-Dong mine")[155] they frequently show young women as energetic actors in their own psychosexual development, rather than as passive objects of male desire. Nor do they seem to experience any guilt about what they do. It is frequently Iseult's ingenuity (not to say duplicity) that saves Tristan as Olwen saves Culhwch and plots with him to overthrow her father. In the story of Iseult too it is the woman who first declares her love, as in the Irish story of Derdriu and Naoise, for instance:

> When Naoise was out there alone therefore [Derdriu] slipped out quickly to him and made as though to pass him and not recognise him. "That is a fine heifer going by", he said. She said, "The heifers grow big where there are no bulls." "You have the bull of the province all to yourself", he said, "the King of Ulster". "Of the two," she said, "I'd pick a game young bull like you." "You couldn't," he said, "there is Cathbad's prophecy" (that Derdriu's love would bring death and disaster). "Are you rejecting me?" she said, "I am," he said. Then she rushed at him and caught the two ears of his head. "Two ears of shame and mockery," she said, "if you don't take me with you." "Woman, leave me alone," he said. "You will do it," she said, binding him.[156]

Derdriu's choice, like Iseult's, has tragic consequences but she faces them with courage. Misogynistic attitudes expressed by male characters or monkish redactors are not surprising: what is surprising is that so many strong and resourceful female characters have survived in the literature. For girls the developmental obstacle is usually identified as male power, either the father or some older man whom she is expected to marry, without of course her own wishes being consulted, as Iseult's were not. Though such heroines are often seen as a threat to the established male order, what Lacan calls "the name of the Father", they are sometimes, like Derdriu, accorded a

---

155 *Ibid.*, p. 55.
156 Kinsella, T., *op. cit.*, p. 12.

tragic dignity: taken as a whole the stories express male ambivalence: women may be both desirable and dangerous, subversive of the very order which it is their specific role to preserve.

As Julia Kristeva has pointed out, the necessity for the girl to fit into the symbolic (male) order while at the same time seeking a sexual object of a different gender to their first loved object, the mother (in the boys' case of course the two are most commonly the same) imposes an enormous burden.[157] The Celtic stories fit more neatly into a post-modern feminist construct than they do into the Freudian model, but no psychoanalytic paradigm really fits. It is in any case evident that there is more to these stories than romantic love. Indeed it is hard to see how they could have survived so long if they had not expressed some fundamental truth about the way people are.

Castle Dor

Castle Dor provides an interesting twentieth century take on the legend of Tristan and Iseult. Sir Arthur Quiller-Couch (who wrote as "Q") was a Cornish critic and novelist, author of *The Astonishing History of Troy Town*, *The Splendid Spur*, *The Ship of Stars*, and many other books.[158] He was Professor of English at Cambridge and editor of the first *Oxford Book of English Verse*. Shortly before his death in 1944 he began a novel based on the story of Tristan and Iseult, and his daughter later recalled that the story was "born in the early 1920s".[159] Looking over the unfinished manuscript in 1959 she decided to ask her friend Daphne du Maurier to complete it, and it was finally published in 1962.[160]

The novel is firmly set in the countryside around the Fowey river, which Quiller-Couch knew and loved. It was on a visit to his friends Mr and Mrs Santo of Lantyan that he was struck by the corre-spondence between the setting of Béroul's *Romance of Tristan* and the local setting around Fowey. This inspired him to rewrite the legend,

---

157 See Kristeva, J. (19889). *Black Sun*. New York, Columbia University Press.
158 See Drabble, M., *op. cit.*, p. 832.
159 See Quiller-Couch, A. and Du Maurier, D. (1962, reprint 1979). *Castle Dor*. London, Pan Books.
160 See also Symonc, A. C. (2003). 'Quiller-Couch on Tristan and Yseut'. *An Baner Kernewok 112*, May 2003.

setting it in the nineteenth century. This it seems was intended to link the medieval romanticism of Béroul with the romantic construct of nineteenth-century Cornwall, popularized by du Maurier herself, and an important part of the tourist industry. This romantic perspective ensures that the nineteenth-century background is imperfectly realized, and there is little sense of the huge social and economic changes which Cornwall was undergoing at this time.

Castle Dor itself is very patchy, and one can see why Quiller-Couch was reluctant to complete and publish it. The parts of Tristan and Iseult are taken by Amyot, a Breton onion-seller, and Linnet Lewarno, newly married to the landlord of the Rose and Anchor at Fowey, an unconvincing parallel to King Mark in the original. Amyot himself is a cipher, and it is hard to see how he could become the object of passionate love. The idea that the story recurs throughout history with the same tragic force holds the story together but is rather laboured. As Dr Carfax reflects:

> What was happening now had happened a hundred times before; that the scene between them was a sickening repetition of others known too well; that he was in fact that very husband whose disparity in years between him and his bride was bringing him through jealous rage to the borderline of madness. Not once, twice, thrice but a dozen times had she been unfaithful to him, yet always the proof of guilt was turned, and he, the accuser, made to seem accused.[161]

At such times the writing has a genuine power but all too often the parallels between past and present seem mechanical and rather obvious.[162]

One of the ways this is done is through Dr Carfax and his French visitor, Monsieur Ledru, supposedly based on the great Celtic scholar Joseph Loth, whose ongoing discussions on Béroul's topography are meant to illuminate the story, but often hold up the action. This occurs mostly in Quiller-Couch's half of the book: on

---

161 Quiller-Couch and Du Maurier, *op. cit.*, p. 146.

162 Alan Garner uses the story of Lleu and Blodeuwedd in a similar way in his brilliant 1967 novel 'The Owl Service', but it is done more effectively there.

the whole du Maurier's skilful manipulation of atmosphere achieves the desired effect more economically. Du Maurier writes:

> The only enemy was time; not the gathering dusk that would encompass them, nor the passing hours, but the freakish, ghostly time that had come upon them out of the buried past, holding them all in thrall[163]

a sentence which nicely captures both the transience of love as we experience it, and the perennial quality of the love story itself.

Alison Light has described du Maurier's "Romantic Toryism" as escape from the "lack-lustre present", and in *Castle Dor* Alan Kent sees the beginnings of an ideological shift towards nationalism: towards the end of her life du Maurier became a member of the nationalist party Mebyon Kernow.[164] Kent has also claimed that:

> more scholars and writers now acknowledge the fact that the writing of historical romance has been highly effective in offering to Cornish and non-Cornish readerships particular images of Cornish identity, history and difference, while also offering a continuum from numerous aspects of both structure and theme from Cornish literary history.[165]

The Otherworldly Lover

The story of Tristan and Iseult contains many motifs which anticipate later literature and folklore, both in Cornwall and in the wider Celtic world. It is itself "interceltic", like the lives of so many Cornish saints: Tristan journeys from his home in Lyonesse to serve Mark in Cornwall, finds a lover in Ireland and a wife in Brittany, and his story has since gone global. The voyage itself is a characteristically "Celtic motif", the "Immram" of Irish storytelling, the Quest for the Grail, the voyages of Prince Madoc, the voyages of Bran and Máel Dúin, of Brendan, the wandering saint, whose

---

163 *Op. cit.*, p. 225.
164 See Light, A. (1991). *Forever England: Femininity, Literature and Conservatism between the Wars*. London, Routledge. And Kent, *op. cit.*, p. 183.
165 *Ibid.*, p. 244.

adventures also fascinated medieval Europe.[166] The search for the otherworld is also a search for the ultimate reality of this world, the truth about oneself, and the story of Tristan and Iseult begins and ends with a voyage.

Iseult herself has a variety of otherworldly characteristics. She is "the lady with the hair of gold" whose hair is carried over the sea by the swallows, "a woman's hair long and fine and shining like a beam of light",[167] reminding one of Olwen and Niamh of the Golden Hair. She is also a magical healer, like the Cornish saints: she heals Tristan when he is poisoned by the dragon, and is coming to heal him when he dies at the end of the story. Niamh was a woman of the Sidhe or fairy folk who seduced Oisín and led him to Tír na nÓg, the magical otherworld where no-one grows older: when he eventually returns to Ireland he ages suddenly and dies. Niamh means "brightness" and "radiance", and "Gráinne" has a similar root.[168] In the stories known in Ireland as "elopements" the male protagonists often have supernatural associations also: Diarmuid is son of the god Donn and Noisiu has the ability to increase the yield of cows, like the Tuatha Dé Danann, the Irish gods. In the French and German versions of *Tristan* the hero is a son of "Blanchfleur", who has been compared to the Greek goddess of love Aphrodite, the "Flowerlady".[169] Though it seems late in the day for Max Müller's solar mythology some have seen in the symbolism of these stories the perennial battle between winter and spring, light and darkness.[170] However, it is evident that Iseult has something of the "otherworldly lover" about her, and it may be that the story does derive from some early mythological core. This of course does not delimit its meaning, though it might enrich it.

The women of the Sidhe, the fairy women of Ireland, were both beautiful and dangerous. They were called the Sidhe after the mounds in which they lived, which were gateways to the otherworld.

166 See O'Donaghue, A. (1893, reprint 1994). *Lives and Legends of St. Brendan.* Felinfach, Llanerch.

167 Redier, *op. cit.*, p. 225.

168 See MacKillop, *op. cit.*, p. 306.

169 Rees, A. and Rees, B. (1961). *Celtic Heritage*. London, Thames and Hudson, p. 293.

170 *Ibid.*, pp. 282-7.

It was believed that the Tuatha Dé Danann went to live in these fairy forts after their defeat by the Milesians, the ancestors of the Irish people. Though invisible most of the time, the people of the Sidhe do sometimes interfere in the affairs of human beings, and it is unwise to cross them. As we have seen Niamh's seduction of Oisín has disastrous consequences for him, and the "Leannán Sidhe" or fairy lover is a common theme in Gaelic literature and folklore.

At the other end of the social scale from the lordly Tuatha Dé Danann was the Manx Lhiannin Shee:

Once a man was going to Cregneeish when he was followed by a fairy woman, or Lhiannin shee. She tried to get him to turn around and look at her, which would giver her power over him, but he covered his eyes until she turned away. Then he watched and saw her hide the chest she was carrying underneath a bush. He came back the following day and carried the chest home. When he opened it he found a treasure of gold and a long tress of shining golden hair. He hid it under an elder tree to keep it safe from the fairy woman who looked through his window every night, sighing plaintively. It occurred to the man that if he got married the fairy woman might leave him alone.

So he went to Iliam Christian's house and asked if he could marry his daughter, but the old man said she was promised to Juan Tease, who was well off. The man dug up his treasure and showed it to Iliam, hoping to impress him. Old Iliam was uneasy about the "mermaid's hair", which he considered unlucky, and said that if the gold was sold the man could marry Joaney, which he did:

But that night the lhiannin shee came looking in at the window, and sighing as if her heart would break.

Joaney asked what the noise was, but he said it was a curlew calling.

But later the fairy woman came when Joaney was away nursing her mother, and when he saw her beautiful face the man got up and followed her. He spent seven years with her but it seemed only a day to him, as it did with Oisín in Tír na nÓg. When he came home again he saw Joaney rocking the cradle. "Don't you know me?" he asked, but she said her husband had drowned seven years ago, and that she waited five years for him, and then married Juan. The man caught sight of his reflection in the mirror and saw that he had grown old and grey: he also saw the face of the fairy woman, and with a cry he ran away into the night. And the fairy gold melted away into withered leaves.

> They say too, that it would be better for a man to jump over the edge of the broogh and be drowned, than to look at the face of the lhinnin shee, for there's no more peace at him, but wandering, wandering forever. For the face of the fairy woman is lovelier than a dream, and lonelier than a sea-bird's cry.[171]

This haunting little story, though perhaps based on "Oisín's visit to the land of Youth" has more in common with Cornish folklore than with the court of King Mark and the conventions of courtly love. Nonetheless these folktales are often moving and the unhappiness of all three characters in the Mark story recalls the fate of the main characters in the old triadic tales. Even some details, such as the golden hair and the premature ageing of the hero recall the earlier stories. It may be that some folktales contain dim memories of the tragedies of Oisín, Tristan and Iseult, and the rest. The Celtic aristocracies which had supported the old "high storytelling" were destroyed by the English invasions, and storytellers then had to adapt or create new stories for less sophisticated audiences, and this happened earlier in Cornwall than elsewhere, which may explain the shortage of Arthurian material. Because of this it has been necessary to draw on analogues from the other Celtic countries, though this does have the advantage of highlighting the connections between them.

In Cornwall itself the otherworldly lover was most often a mermaid such as the "very beautiful and richly attired lady" who attended divine service in Zennor church and enticed Mathey Trewella to her undersea home from which he never returned.[172] Often though mermaids are depicted taking vengeance on people who threaten or

---

171 Broome, D. (1951). *Fairy Tales from the Isle of Man.* Douglas, Norris Press.
172 Bottrell, *op. cit.*

harm them, like the mermaids of Seaton and Padstow. In Bottrell's story of the Mermaid of Lizard Point the "merrymaid" charms a man called Lutey with tales about her underwater home, a veritable Celtic otherworld:

> Come with me love and see the beauty of the mermaid's dwellings. Yet the ornaments with which we take the most delight to embellish our halls and chambers are the noble sons and fair daughters of earth, whom the wind and waves send in foundered ships to our abodes. Come, I will show you thousands of handsome bodies so embalmed, in a way only known to ourselves, with choice salts and rare spices, that they look more beautiful than when they breathed, as you will say when you see them reposing on beds of amber, coral and pearl decked with rich stuffs, and surrounded by heaps of silver and gold...[173]

though this is not so much Tír na nÓg as the Land of the Dead, and Lutey is less interested in the embalmed corpses than in the "casks of brandy, kegs of Hollands, pipes of wine and puncheons of rum" which find their way to the undersea land from the sunken ships, and this does recall the feasting which was typical of the old Celtic otherworld, as well as reflecting the desires of impoverished audiences. Certainly the rounded sentences in this passage do not record the mode of speech of Bottrell's working-class informant. Collectors had a tendency to polish their stories to make them more acceptable to a middle-class metropolitan audience. Such stories seem often to be driven by wish-fulfilment, just as stories of other-worldly love were often driven by frustration and sexual fantasy: this is clear in the story of

The Fairy Widower

Once in Towednack there lived a pretty girl called Jenny Permuen, who had romantic ideas in her head, and was attractive to the local young men. One day she met a handsome man who was a stranger

173 *Ibid.*, p. 65.

to her: he was a widower and offered her a job nursing his little boy. He confesses that he finds her attractive:

> "do you think a young widower could pass through Towednack and not be struck by such a pretty girl? Besides," he said, "I watched you one day dressing your hair in one of my ponds and stealing some of my sweet-scented violets to put in those lovely tresses …"[174]

Jenny agrees to work for him for a year and a day. The man wipes her eyes with some leaves, and the ground appears to open up, and Jenny finds herself in a beautiful new world, full of "ladies and gentlemen dressed in green and gold". Her new master leads her to a mansion in which all the furniture is made of ivory and pearl, inlaid with gold and emeralds. He introduces her to the child who will be in her care and explains that he is the king of this magical country. Jenny takes care of the child and is happy, though nothing more is said of her relationship with the widower/king.

When her contract expires she wakes up in her own bed in her mother's cottage: she tells everyone what has happened to her but is not believed until an old woman applies a magical test to prove that she was telling the truth. But the story ends sadly. Jenny

> married and was discontented and far from happy. Some said she always pined after the Fairy Widower. Others said they were sure she had misbehaved herself, or she would have brought back lots of gold.[175]

Clearly the otherworld could be a repository for all sorts of desires which could not find expression in ordinary life.

"The Story of Cherry of Zennor" is essentially a variant of "The Fairy Widower". When Cherry was sixteen years old her friend was given a new dress, and boasted that he had several sweethearts who followed her home: Cherry's parents could not afford to buy her new clothes. One morning she tied her clothes into a bundle and went off looking for work so she could earn some money. She walked and

---

174 Hunt, *op. cit.*, pp. 113-18.
175 *Ibid.*, pp. 120-26.

walked until she came to the crossroads on the Lady Downs, where she sat down and cried for homesickness. When a "handsome gentleman" passed, she told him she had decided to return to Zennor. He said he had been looking for "a nice clean girl" to keep house for him and look after his little boy so she agreed to go with him. When they came to a stream the gentleman put his arm around her waist and carried her over. The path "seemed to be going rapidly downhill" until they reached a beautiful garden with flowers of every colour, and a little boy came out accompanied by an old woman, whom the widower introduced as his late wife's grandmother, Prudence.

They went into the house which was even more beautiful than the garden. Cherry ate a wonderful supper and went to sleep in the same room as her little charge. Prudence warned her to keep her eyes closed all night, and not to speak to the child: she was to get up at daybreak, take the child into the garden and wash him, then anoint his eyes with a special ointment, being careful not to touch her own eyes with it. She also had to work in the kitchen but was told not to go anywhere else in the house out of curiosity. One day Jenny decided to rub some of the ointment into her own eyes, after she discovered that the little boy seemed to see things that were invisible to her. The ointment made her eye burn, so she ran to the pool to wash it off. At the bottom of the pool she saw hundreds of little people playing, and there was her master, as small as the others: he came back to the house in the evening, looking his usual self. Cherry kept repeating her experiment until one day she saw her master kissing one of the little ladies. The next day her master stayed at home, and when he attempted to kiss Cherry as he usually did she slapped his face and told him to kiss his little lady, and so he discovered that she had used the magic ointment. Sadly he told her that she would have to go home, and he led her uphill, back to her own world, and the story ends with a characteristic note of sadness and loss:

> They say Cherry was never afterwards right in her head, and on moonlit nights, until she died, she would wander on to the Lady Downs to look for her master.

Searching behaviour of this kind is of course a classic sign of grief. A similar story was told of Anne Jefferies, a St Teath woman who was born in 1626 and is supposed to have died in 1698.[176] Anne too was transported to a wonderful land, with

> temples and palaces of gold and silver. Trees laden with fruits and flowers. Lakes full of gold and silver fish and the air full of birds of the sweetest song, and the most brilliant colours..."

There she found a fairy lover, and "lovingly did they pass the time, and Anne desired that this should continue for ever", but they were attacked by the other fairies who were jealous. Her lover was wounded, someone touched her eyes and Anne was transported back to the real world. Anne was a real person who claimed to have met the fairies and to have been given healing powers by them. In 1646 she was accused of witchcraft and sent to Bodmin Gaol by John Tregeagle, himself a demonic figure in Cornish legend, where she was starved and tortured but miraculously sustained by her supernatural friends. Eventually she was released and continued her life as a healer: then she married a man called William Warner, later dying of old age.[177]

All these stories end on a sad note and none employ the conventional rhetoric of romantic love, but beneath the polite circumventions of the collectors, the sexual issue emerges quite clearly. The fairy worlds of the stories also allow the human visitors to transcend the limitations of class, to be loved by "ladies and gentlemen" above their own social levels. Although they obviously embody the fantasies of lonely and overworked servant girls, they may also refer back to an older, more realistic view of love, one that acknowledges its destructive aspects as well as its creative ones; and this is the tension that has always made the Cornish story of Tristan, Iseult and King Mark so compelling. In a completely different context, that of early Gaelic love poetry. Seán Ó Tuama writes of:

---

176 For what follows see Hunt, *ibid.*, pp. 127-129.

177 Hunt gives an interesting letter about Anne from her employer Moses Bitt to the Bishop of Gloucester, who was interested in her case. See Hunt, *op. cit.*, Appendix K.

the tendency not to see human love as an absolute, an ideal vision abstracted out of life (as in medieval European poetry) but as a troublesome gift or overwhelming moment of desire at the centre of the mundane routines of life.[178]

Perhaps this too is part of the Cornish vision which underlies both "The Fairy Widower" and the original tragedy of Tristan and Iseult.

---

178 Ó Tuama, S. (1989). "The Lineage of Gaelic Love Poetry from the Earlist Times." In O'Driscoll, R. (ed.) (1982). *The Celtic Consciousness*. New York, George Braziller, p. 289.

Chapter 4

The Saints of Cornwall

The Saints of Cornwall

Next to the *Ordinalia* the most impressive surviving fragments of Middle Cornish literature are the two saints' plays, *Beunans Meriasek* or "The Life of St Meriasek" and *Bewnans Ke* or "The Life of St Kea":[179] it seems likely that there were once many more such plays, but that they were destroyed at the Reformation along with the Latin "Lives" of the saints, which were once kept in every parish church. Nicholas Roscarrock saw a "life" of Saint Columb, virgin and martyr, but this is no longer known.[180] This saint, not to be confused with the great Irish Saint Columba, was martyred by a "Tyrant" (possibly the same "Teudar" who appears in the surviving plays "at a place called Ruthwac, at which place there is a well at this date which beareth her name".[181] The saints' plays were evidently popular throughout Ccornwall in which there were many open-air playing places, along with the more substantial *Ordinalia* trilogy and Robin Hood plays, as well as plays on Old Testament themes such as the lost "Susanna", all of which were acted and produced by local communities, perhaps with the involvement of travelling players.[182]

Alan Kent makes an important point concerning this literature:

> As we have now clearly seen, unlike many of the other Celtic territories during the medieval period, Cornwall's literary energies did not, for the most part, appear to focus on a mythic or heroic Cornish age—as it did in territories such

---

179 See WhitleyStokes, *op. cit.*, and Thomas and Williams, *op. cit.*

180 Orme, N. (ed.) (1992). *Nicholas Roscarrock's 'Lives of the Saints'.* Devon and Cornwall Record Society.

181 *Ibid.*, p. 67.

182 For the background see Alan Kent's *The Theatre of Cornwall: Space, Place, Performance* (2010).

as Wales and Ireland, but rather, the focus was on a merging of European-wide biblical narrative on to Cornish experience. As we might expect, considering its close cultural development with Cornwall, Brittany was the only other territory to hold such a fully developed continuum.[183]

This context is helpful and reflects a Cornish desire to remain part of Europe as a way of resisting English assimilation and cultural appropriation.

The Life of St Kea

The survival of at least some of this material testifies to the respect in which Cornish saints were held. As does the landscape of Cornwall to this day. Pevsner's famous guide to the buildings of Cornwall for instance lists sixty-nine places named after saints, many of which have legends attached to them and in some cases rituals and cults which precede the Reformation. Many saints had wells, the waters of which were said to possess curative powers, and such beliefs may not be entirely dead: the well at St Cleer was used to cure psychosis by immersion, as was St Ninne's well. St Ludgan's provided healing eyewash, and Jesus Well in Miniver was said to cure whooping cough.[184] This last dedication is near Padstow, ("Petroc's Place") and is uniquely named after Christ himself. In these cases, and countless others, the holy places continued the healing work carried out by the saint in life, for they were all miracle workers: St Petroc and St Nechtan were especially famous for working wonders, and miracles were also associated with Kea and Meriasek, and are depicted in their plays: this was not merely to add dramatic interest—miracles set the seal on sanctity, expressing divine power through the agency of those who were especially chosen by God and sanctified by His holy church.

This phenomenon may go back to the early days of conversion, when working miracles must have been a powerful way of making converts. Though modern readers may find it puzzling, miracles were also a form of preaching. People knew then as they know now

183 Kent (2001), *op. cit.* pp.43-5.
184 See Courtney, M. A. (1998 reprint). *Cornish Feasts and Folklore*. Penzance, Oakmagic, pp. 62-8.

that restoring the dead to life or curing leprosy were not things that
happened in the normal course of events, but they also saw that
miracles expressed the healing power of God and His love for His
people: in this sense they recapitulated the central miracle of Christ's
own resurrection, which we see dramatized in the *Ordinalia*.

Miracles resemble magic, insofar as they transgress the categories
of everyday life in order to effect transformation. Both are otherworldly processes and both imaginatively generate possibilities
denied by reality and the laws of cause and effect. Both are controlled
by gifted individuals, wizards and saints, who possess spiritual power,
and conversion stories sometimes feature a contest between the new
power of the saint and the old power of the wizard or druid. In the
Cornish plays the equivalent is the struggle between the saint and
the tyrant "Teudar", a name probably derived from Theoderic but
containing also a reference to the House of Tudor, which was
deservedly unpopular in Cornwall, and this element of spiritual
rivalry is made explicit in *Bewnans Ké* for instance:

TEUTHARUS
"Ser the thewan, te pen pist
ha pur harlot!
Na gows thymmo vy a Christ,
an raf rybot
a ve maraw
rag e foly i'n crowspryn.
In mes a'm golag omden,
rag nu'm pleg the lavarow."

KELADOCUS
"Eth egus ow cokya
drys peb i'n wlas.
Kin fyrwys mab Marya,
Du mer e ras,
abarth dengys,
der thowgys e tathorhas
e honnyn par del vynnas,
ha'y lel servantes dyspernys." (ll. 299-312)

TEUDAR

"Shut your mouth, you blockhead
and utter scoundrel!
Do not speak to me of Christ,
the worthless ribald
who died
for his folly on the cross.
Be off from my sight,
for your words do not please me."

ST KEA

"You are a being foolish
more than all men in the kingdom.
Though the son of Mary died,
God of great grace,
with respect to his humanity,
by deity he rose from the dead
just as he wished himself,
and his faithful servants redeemed."[185]

The Life of St Kea begins with Kea's voyage across the sea on a stone
(a common motif in Cornish hagiography). He journeys on to the
Forest of Rosewa in Cornwall, and is taken to King Teudar. He tries
to convert the heathen king without success. Kea is then thrown into
prison, where he finds comfort in prayer and is surrounded by a
dazzling light and a sweet smell. He seems impervious to torture, which
infuriates Teudar, who eventually releases him while urging him to
deny Christ and worship "Jovyn" which he of course refuses to do.

Eventually Teudar relents and agrees to give Kea a plot of land in
Rosewa, where he can live a life of prayer provided he does not
preach against the tyrant's own gods. (Several folios are missing from
the manuscript and this is one point of several in which it is difficult
to follow the story.) Kea prays to Christ for water and a well springs
up at his feet. He uses the water to heal a leper, and when he reaches
Rosewa stags appear to pull his plough. Teudar offers to befriend
Kea if he will worship his god Jovyn, but the saint refuses. Teudar

185 Thomas and Williams, *op. cit.*, pp. 30-1.

fears Kea's magical powers, and agrees to give him as much land as he can enclose in the time it takes the king to have a bath. Oubra, a wise woman bewitches Teudar so that he sticks in the bath, giving Kea time to enclose a large tract of land. Teudar appeals his god Jovyn, and there is another gap in the text.

When the play resumes King Arthur addresses an audience of his subjects and courtesies are exchanged, establishing Arthur's status as a powerful and gracious monarch, a legitimate and wise ruler, in contrast to the tyrannical and illegitimate king Teudar. The scene then shifts to the court of the Emperor Lucius Hiberius who complains that though every nation pays him tribute "Arthur the Cornishman" alone refuses to pay. There is another gap and when the story picks up again Arthur announces his intention to defy the emperor. Though owing much to Geoffrey of Monmouth and the conventions of medieval romance Arthur here becomes the Celtic resistance leader of Dark Age history, fighting against foreign encroachment to defend his people's freedom, though he also represented the vestiges of Roman power and authority pitted against barbarian outsiders. The role of St Kea in the plot is unclear because of the fragmentary status of the text.

Lucius threatens to punish Arthur for his defiance and summons allies to his assistance: meanwhile Arthur invades imperial territory. Lucius's army sets off for Gaul to confront him. Arthur says goodbye to his Queen Guinevere and entrusts the kingdom to his nephew Modred:

> "Ow spous gentyl, Guynuwer,
> mos the'n batal me a vyn.
> Gwayt may rylhy the thuver,
> gurthuherow ha myttyn.
> Gweth ve y'th cof
> ha'm noe a ra the rewlya.
> Du roy theugh gul honesta.
> Mos a raf. Ny won a thof." (ll. 2741-48)

> "My noble spouse, Guinevere,
> I will go to battle.

Be sure to do your duty
in the evenings and in the morning.
Keep me in remembrance
and my nephew shall govern you.
May God give you power to do what is seemly.
I depart."[186]

This passage must have been laden with irony for a Cornish audience, aware that Guinevere's disloyalty and Modred's treachery had fatally weakened the British cause and assured an eventual Anglo-Saxon victory.

Just as the dramatist uses references to Cornish topography to create a complex vision that embraces both past and present, local and distant, secular and divine so this scene speaks both to past history and present dilemmas, while also pointing to a possible future redemption. We know from other sources that fourteenth century Cornwall nourished a hope that Arthur would come again to lead in their hour of need, and in the play Arthur exhorts them to

"Keep me in remembrance …
Whether I shall return I know not,"

Modred compels the bishop to crown him king of Britain, a usurpation of illegitimate authority which sets the scene for what follows. When Arthur hears what Modred has done he returns to Britain to set things right. In the meantime Modred has recruited Saxon mercenaries and promised them land in exchange for their support. Arthur and Modred meet in battle and Modred is defeated. Guinevere is expressing remorse for her betrayal, and the play abruptly ends.

A comparison with Albert Le Grand's "Life of St Kea" may help to fill some of the gaps in the play text.[187] According to Le Grand Ke was born in Britain and became a bishop there. The life contains a legend of Ke obtaining a magic bell from Gildas, a bell which rings by itself when he reaches Rosewa. It also includes the story of the saint's journey across the sea on a stone, and the stone itself was

---

186 *Ibid.*, pp. 272-3.
187 *Ibid.*, pp. xii-xxxiv.

pointed out on the banks of the Fal well into the nineteenth century. The treatment of the tyrant Teudar is fuller in the play than it is in the Latin "Life".

Le Grand moves on to the Arthur story which is substantially the same as it is in the play but here Ke, alarmed by Modred's alliance with the pagan Saxons, attempts to mediate between Arthur and his nephew. He fails but does persuade the queen to enter a convent and atone for her sins. This scenario is full of dramatic potential, and it is possible that the Cornish dramatist made use of it, or some earlier version of it. The relation between the two texts, both of which owe much to Geoffrey of Monmouth is unclear.

Thomas and Williams identify "at least two occasions where the text of the play may be following local Cornish tradition rather than Geoffrey of Monmouth.[188] One is the identification of Arthur's court with "Kyllywyk", as it is in the Welsh "Culhwch and Olwen", rather than Caerleon on Usk, the "City of the Legions" as it is in Geoffrey: Kelliwic seems to have been a hill fort at Egloshayle near Padstow. The other occasion is the adoption of the Cornish name for Arthur's famous sword:

> "Saw ny vyth gwyth gweth ys fol,
> pan i'n crennif Calesvol,
> me a'n dyhals." (ll. 3268-70)

> "But he will not dare deeds worse than a fool,
> when I shake it — Excalibur —
> I shall cleave him in two."[189]

The Cornish name marks out the Arthurian storyline as distinctively Cornish and ancient in origin. Pre-dating Geoffrey and the later romances, despite its medieval borrowings—this is indeed "Arthur Cornow", Arthur the Cornishman.

The ambivalence of the play with regard to time (then but also now), and space (there but also here), represents an attempt to connect with the past, in order to generate cultural resistance, and with the outer world of Catholic Europe in order to escape

188 *Ibid.*, p. xxxii.
189 *Ibid.*, pp. 326-7.

Cornwall's provincial deadlock in south-western England, a grip which became even stronger after the Reformation. The appropriation of Dumnonia and then Cornwall itself left no sphere but culture in which the Cornish could express their identity, and much of that was destroyed in the end. The setting of the "mystery plays" made it possible to integrate them into a celebration of identity that was rooted both in the past and in the contemporary life of the community. The Arthurian storyline in *Bewnans Ke* also roots it in the borderland between myth and history as well as addressing the dominant literary and religious concerns of the European mainland. And this was no accident. As Philip Payton reminds us:

> the co-option of the Arthurian tradition by the British Project was matched (like the Europeanisation of Tristan and Iseult) by its adoption by continental romancers who wove tales of Arthur as medieval sovereign. Here stories of kingship and chivalry, of courtly love and the Holy Grail, produced a further "Vision of Albion", a continental view of these islands in which Cornwall's distinctive place in the "Matter of Britain" was made plain. It is no coincidence that most European languages have their own word for Cornwall (but never for Hampshire or Rutland), as though it were a Scotland or a Wales, so that Cornwall's status is not merely of British but rather wider European significance.[190]

Drama, in the absence of other independent institutions which might have kept the dream of national autonomy alive, helped to nurture both memory and identity, at a time when both were problematic.

The Life of Meriasek

Before the *Bewnans Ke* was discovered, at the beginning of the twenty-first century, subversive tendencies had already been noticed in the *Beunans Meriasek*, a text which had been known and studied since 1872.

---

190 Payton, *op. cit.*, pp. 75-6.

To mention Cornish nationhood today in modern England is to invite derision. This is for two reasons. The first is defensive: we laugh at people and ideas which are different because we experience them as a threat to our ways of understanding the world. And secondly we have absorbed the Victorian concept of the nation-state as a good thing with our mothers' milk. So Cornwall is nothing but a charming holiday destination because that is what we need it to be. It comes then as a shock to realize that the Cornish themselves have never accepted their incorporation into south-west England.

Alan Kent has argued that:

> This relationship between the colonizer and colonized is filled with considerable tension. For the Cornish what cannot be explicitly acknowledged is their possession of an alternative language, literature and culture.[191]

Meriasek

To acknowledge these differences would sabotage the ideal of the unitary nation state. This tension is expressed in medieval Cornish drama, especially in the saints' plays, but it also explains why it took so long to recognize the subversive subtext in *Beunans Meriasek*. The great Irish scholar Whitley Stokes first edited and published the text in 1872, only three years after it was first discovered.[192] The play itself seems to have been staged in the immediate aftermath of the 1497 rebellion when the Bodmin lawyer Thomas Flamank and the St Keverne blacksmith Michael Joseph An Gof, "the smith" led a Cornish army into England. After fighting with great courage the Cornish surrendered at Blackheath and their leaders were hung, drawn and quartered at Tyburn. *Beunans Meriasek* celebrated the life of a saint well known in both Cornwall and Brittany. Philip Payton has seen the play as a subversive document:

> At the very least, the theme of tyranny and the choice of Teudar (perhaps a reference to Henry Tudor?) would have struck a Cornish audience as particularly apposite, while the specific desire to stage the play in 1504 may have been a

---

191 Kent (2000) *op. cit.*, p.44.
192 Whitley Stokes (1872), *op. cit.*

good indication of the strength of Cornish feeling at that time.[193]

Not very much is known about Meriasek, who was known in Brittany under the name of Meriadoc. He seems to have been Welsh in origin, though his birthplace and dates are unknown. The copying of the play was completed in 1504, by "Rad Ton", whose identity is uncertain. The piece had been composed at an earlier date, but was obviously considered relevant to conditions in the early sixteenth century.[194] The story has much in common with other late medieval saints' lives—the conflict with a pagan persecutor and the healing miracles are not untypical. The Latin *Life* of the saint does not specifically link him to Cornwall, which may suggest that his Cornish travels were added to the story after his cult had been transplanted from Brittany. The play also contains episodes from the legendary life of St Silvester, and it has been criticized for failing to unite its disparate elements. Brian Murdoch though discerns a number of overreaching themes:

> The principal of these are the relations between church and state, the combating of evil and the conversion of unbelievers, and the role of saints and the clergy as intercessors, with special emphasis on the Virgin."[195]

Saints' plays are rather rare in English and those that are known concern biblical saints. The Sylvester episode begins with the Emperor Constantine's persecution of the Christians and the burial of the martyrs by Pope Silvester, as Constantine is stricken by leprosy.[196] He is advised to seek a cure by bathing in the blood of three thousand children. But Constantine takes pity on the children and sets them free. The Emperor sees saints Peter and Paul in a vision, and decides to become a Christian and to establish

193 Payton, P. (1992). 'A Concealed Envy against the English', a note on the aftermath of the 1497 rebellions in Cornwall. In *Cornish Studies 1* (ed. Payton). See also Alan Kent's helpful discussion in Kent, op. cit., pp. 45-8.

194 Murdoch, *op. cit.*, pp. 99-126.

195 *Ibid.*, p. 102.

196 Whitley Stokes, *op. cit.*, p. vi.

Christianity throughout his empire. Back in Cornwall Teudar is defeated by the Duke and Meriasek performs a series of miracles. Sylvester appoints him Bishop of Vannes when the old bishop dies, and after initially refusing the honour he eventually accepts. In an unusual episode the only son of a certain woman goes to serve King Massen, who may be the famous "Massen Wledig" of Welsh legend, and is captured by yet another heathen tyrant who attacks and kills the rightful king. The mother appeals to the Blessed Virgin Mary to save her son. Mary disregards her prayer and the tyrant orders the son to be executed.

In revenge the mother steals the effigy of the Christ-child from the statue of the Virgin, whereupon the real Virgin descends from Heaven and restores the living son to his mother, who returns the baby to the statue. In contrast, we see the tyrant's men holding a black mass which the dramatist uses to point up the consequences of sin. The focus shifts back to St Meriasek who performs more miracles, including the cure of a madman. In a dramatic climax Sylvester kills a dragon. As always in medieval hagiography this is a metaphor for the victory of faith over unbelief, as Sylvester says:

> "Dre voth crist arluth avan
> an dragan me a ra guan
> dregen in pov na relle
> may welle myns us in rome
> ihesu crist a bev ry dome
> ha gul kepar del vynne." (ll. 4003-8

> "Through the will of Lord Christ above
> The dragon I will pierce
> So that she may do no hurt in the country.
> So that all that are in Rome may see
> Jesus Christ owns (the right) of giving doom,
> And doth as he will."[197]

This religious element is of course predominant, though it is not without subversive implications, firstly because it links Cornwall to

197 *Ibid.*, p. 124.

the wider Christian world outside England, at the point when England is about to secede from that world; and secondly because it is framed and presented in a distinctively Cornish way: so Brian Murdoch identifies the common theme of injustice, but in the Cornish plays it is quite specifically injustice arising out of illegitimate rule, particularly the rule of the Teudars in the two saints' plays. The wrong done to the mother's son, for instance, is done by a tyrant whose rule is invalid because he is a pagan. Constantine has already converted the empire to Christianity. Significantly, the tyrant condemns the boy to the same fate as Flamank and An Gof:

> "Hov geylers golsovugh wy
> me a charg wat beyn tenna
> boys na dewes na regh ry
> then guas a ruk vi orna
> the preson pur eredy
> an vorov rum lel ena
> me a vyn prest y cregy
> y quartrona hay denna. (ll. 3601-8)

> How jailers, hearken ye!
> I charge on pain of drawing,
> Neither food nor drink give ye
> To the lad whom I ordered
> To prison right readily.
> To-morrow, by my loyal soul,
> I will hang him,
> Quarter him, and draw him."[198]

It is quite possible that some in the audience had fought with An Gof and Flamank, and these lines must have had a powerful impact. The Cornish rising though fuelled by many grievances, was provoked by new taxation to fight a Scottish war, which seemed both unjust and irrelevant to Cornwall, imposed by a monarch whose authority over Cornwall was at least questionable. It is known that

198 *Ibid.*, pp. 208-9.

the Cornish were still in an insurrectionary mood after the executions:

> Henry's intention was to send the bodies of Angove and Flamank back to Cornwall for public display as a terrible warning of the consequences of treason—a normal piece of ritual accompanying fifteenth-century rebellions. But hearing of the continued "unquiet and boiling disaffection" in Cornwall in the summer of 1497 this was not deemed the wisest course of action.[199]

Though expressing disaffection in public would be risky, a codified expression of resistance in Cornish in front of a sympathetic audience might have felt safe, especially in a context which was theologically sound, it is interesting too that the dramatist chose two saints' plays to convey his message. It suggests that local saints were associated with Cornish distinctiveness and that their cults were a source of communal solidarity (as can still be seen at the Breton "pardons"). The large number of place-names derived from saints may suggest the same thing. It is evident too that these two surviving plays share the same underlying concerns, and reflect a coded debate about the situation in Cornwall, provoked by or perhaps even leading to the rebellions of 1497. That these issues were discussed at Glasney College, where the plays were written, seems likely, and their presence in the plays shows that they were matters for concern within the wider Cornish-speaking community.

High Days and Holidays
That the Cornish valued their saints is well known, and faced with attempts to replace Cornish church dedications with "foreign" saints, the Cornish re-established or even invented new saints to whom to dedicate their churches—St Keynwynus at Kenwyn and St Ludwanud at Ludgvan for instance are wholly fictitious, and many churches were rebuilt in the early modern period.[200] Throughout the Middle Ages and beyond parishes celebrated their saints' feast-days. The tinners particularly celebrated St Piran's Day in some style

199 Deacon, *op. cit.*, p. 67.
200 Payton, *op. cit.*, p. 99

even though it was frowned on in Methodist times. In 1927 Hamilton Jenkin referred to the name of the feast, which:

> Only remained until recently in the term "Perraner" which, used as a reproach to those whose footsteps were festive rather than steady, showed clearly enough the level to which the saint's day had sunk before its observance ceased altogether.

The feast was a commemoration of the first smelting of tin in Cornwall, the banner of St Peran, with its white cross on a black ground being, according to Gilbert's perhaps far-fetched statement, an allusion to the black ore and white metal of tin.[201]

As we have seen. Though St Piran's Day seems to have been kept widely across west Cornwall, most Cornish saints had a local celebrity and their feasts celebrated the history and identity of the community. Richard Carew in his 1602 survey of Cornwall describes some of the festivities which took place in Cornish parishes in his time, the "harvest dinners", "church ales" and:

> the solemnising of their parish church's dedication which they term their saint's feast … kept upon the dedication day by every householder of the parish, within his own doors, each entertaining such foreign acquaintance as will not fail, when their like turn cometh about to requite him with the like kindness.[202]

These feasts were clearly convivial occasions which brought people together to celebrate a shared identity and a shared memory. So too were the plays, and it is interesting that Carew mentions the drama alongside the feast in his account, though he does not describe an actual performance. The first day of *Beunans Meriasek* ends with an invocation of community, centred on the saint:

---

201 Hamilton Jenkin, A. K. (1927). *The Cornish Miner*. London, Allen and Unwin, p. 130.
202 Carew, R. (2000). *Survey of Cornwall 1602*. Redruth, Tamar Rocks, pp. 80-1.

Peys warberth myns os omma
bevnans meryasek yma
parte thyugh hythyv disquethys
dugh am II. a dermen
han remenant in certen
dre gras du a veth guelys

Evugh oll gans an guary
ny a vyn agis pesy
a luen golon
wy agis beth gor ha gruek
banneth crist ha meryasek
banneth maria cambron
pybugh menstrels colonnek
may hyllyn donsia dyson. (ll. 2499-2512)

Peace altogether all that are here!
Meriasek's Life is
In part to you set forth to-day.
Come ye on the second day in time,
And the remainder, certainly
Through God's grace shall be seen.

Drink ye all with the play,
We will beseech you
With a full heart.
Ye shall have, man and woman,
The blessing of Mary of Camborne.
Pipe ye, hearty minstrels,
That we may be able to dance forthwith.[203]

The last verse recalls the popular cult of the Blessed Virgin, Mary of Camborne: a common motif. The Virgin plays an important role in the action of the play, and is both a local and a universal figure linking the world of the audience with the otherworld of Christ and the saints in Heaven, and this is expressed in her function as an intercessor between the human race and God: this is of course

203 Whitley Stokes, *op. cit.*, pp. 143-5.

traditional Catholic teaching. This passage in the play clearly establishes it as a convivial social event, among other things, and this impression is reinforced by the final verses at the end of Day Two:

> "Dywhy banneth meryasek
> ha maria cambron wek
> banneth an abesteleth
> evugh oll gans an guary
> ny a vyn agis pesy
> kyns moys an plaeth.
>
> Pyboryon wethugh in scon
> my a vyn ketep map bron
> moys the donsya
> eugh bo tregugh
> wolcum vethugh
> kyn fewy sythen omma. (ll. 4557-4568)
>
> To you the blessing of Meriasek,
> And of sweet Mary of Camborne,
> The blessing of the apostles!
> Drink ye all with the play
> We will beseech you
> Before going from the place.
>
> Pipers, blow at once.
> We will, every son of the breast,
> Go to dance.
> Go ye or stay
> Welcome ye shall be,
> Though ye be a week here."[204]

It is clear that the feast days shared something of this conviviality. St Piran himself was traditionally associated with drinking, and according to the cost-book of Great Work mine in Breage for the years 1759-1764, his tradition was kept up there by the miners of Breage and Germoe, who

---

204 *Ibid.*, pp. 264-5.

still retained the observance of St Perran Feast and in March of each year a regular entry appears in the accounts of one shilling to the men and sixpence to the boys "allowance for Perran tide". No doubt the miners of this outlying district retained many old-fashioned customs when they had ceased to be observed elsewhere.[205]

Though earlier writers tended to dismiss such practices as mere self-indulgence, they clearly helped to maintain social cohesion as did the performances and celebrations at the *plen an gwary*.

Historically, Piran seems to have been the Irishman Ciarán of Saigir (the Gaelic "k" sound corresponding to "p" in Cornish): the Irish had seventeen saints called Ciarán, so it is hard to be sure, as is the case with so many early saints. As we saw in comparing the lives of St Kea and St Meriasek, the same biographical motifs tend to recur, which is another source of confusion. Hagiographies were often written centuries after their subjects had died, and real biographical details have been forgotten or embroidered. Writers naturally filled in the gaps with material borrowed from the lives of other saints, which met conventional expectations. Hagiographers were concerned to meet the needs of their own time, and not at all with historical accuracy as we would define it. Such being the case attempting to reconstruct a saint as a historical personage of the fifth or sixth century from a late medieval hagiography is surely futile. What is important is what the stories tell us about the thoughts and feelings of the people who transmitted them down the generations.

Piran is patron of three different parishes in Cornwall, and his cult is also found in Brittany and Wales.[206] He or his followers built the little stone chapel at Perranzabuloe, recently recovered from the sand, with which his name has been associated and which is undoubtedly of an early date: there was a chapel dedicated to Piran on Shoemarket Street in Cardiff before the Reformation. Whether all these dedications refer to the same person, and whether Piran actually was Ciarán, and, if so, which one, is a matter of conjecture, though his importance to the Cornish people is not. A. K. Hamilton Jenkins tells us that:

---

205 Doble, *op. cit.*, Part Four, p. 26.
206 *Ibid*, p. 3.

As late as 1866 the alluvial tin "streamers" of east Cornwall were still in the habit of keeping a number of feasts and holidays peculiar to themselves. Among these may be mentioned "Paul's Pitcher Day" on the eve of Paul's tide (January 24th), Freday in Lido (March 1st) and "Picrous Day (second Thursday before Christmas). The latter feast falls on the same day as "Chewidden" (Cornish "De yew widn", White Thursday) on which, according to the tradition of the western men, tin was first smelted. It may be noted too that Freday in Lido very nearly corresponds with St Piran's Day.[207]

Tin smelting, which was the basis of economic life in Cornwall was celebrated and transformed into legend, the legend of St Piran whose flag symbolized it. It is also associated with the Holy Visit of Christ and Joseph of Arimathea and in folklore with the arrival of the mysterious culture-bearer, Jack the Tinkeard who teaches Tom how to dress the tin. In each case the precious knowledge comes from a numinous stranger from a distant land, and is then passed on and celebrated through the ages, at Morvah Fair for instance, from generation to generation—Christ and Joseph came from Palestine, Piran from Ireland, and "Jack" from Dartmoor.

Cornish and Welsh tradition tells of many saints arriving from distant lands, especially the family of Brychan, an Irish/Welsh king who gave his name to Brocknockshire, and who seems to have flourished in the fifth century.[208] He was said to have had forty-nine children, twenty-four sons and twenty-five daughters, all of them saints. Many of them were hermits in Devon and Cornwall, though many of the surviving names are obscure or clearly spurious. Entries in Borlase's list include:

> Endeliant—a name which we have seen to be fictitious, not mentioned until the thirteenth century. The real founder of the church of Endellion was not of the Brychan family at all.

207 Hamilton Jenkin, *op. cit.*, p. 26-7.
208 See Borlase, W. C. (1893). *The Age of the Saints*. Truro, Joseph Pollard, p. 146.

Menfre—A name probably meant for St Minver of whom nothing is known.

Wesent—unknown.

Wymp—St Veep, as Dr Borlase conjectures, or possibly Gwennap. The real saint seems to have been unknown."[209]

as well as more substantial characters, such as Saints Nectanus, Teath, and Maben. But though individual identities may be doubtful it is possible that the legend of Brychan's children does, as Baring-Gould conjectured, retain a memory of the Irish invasion of north Cornwall which took place early in the sixth century. More fundamentally it embodies the ancient myth of the stranger from another world who comes bearing wisdom, or skills previously unknown. This theme occurs in the stories of Lugh Lamhfhada in Ireland and of the poet-seer Taliesin in Wales. Visitors from the otherworld play a significant part in Cornish folktale, as the knockers and spriggans who turn our own world upside down for instance, and such visitors are not always benign. But visitors from otherworlds can be agents of transformation, changing the way we think and feel, with unforeseen consequences. Iseult comes to Cornwall from an otherworldly Ireland of healing magic and love potions, and turns the court upside down. In this sense the otherworldly visitor functions as a catalyst, bringing out the desires and tensions which are already there, as the tin is there below the Cornish ground, waiting to be smelted and shaped.

Not all the Cornish saints came from Wales or Ireland. Some, such as Winwaloe and Wethenor came from the Dumnonian royal family and are remembered in church dedications, forming a link with the Celtic southwest in its days of independence. Some of these seem to have been active in the fight to preserve that independence. Gereint fab Erbin, "who is called a saint", died fighting his enemies in the woodlands of Devon: he had founded Saint Gerrans in Roseland. An englyn about him, apparently a fragment from a lost cycle of poems, survives from medieval Wales:

---

209 *Ibid.*, pp. 148-51.

When Geraint was born the doors of Heaven were
    opened,
Christ gave that which was prayed for:
A comely form, Britain's glory.
Let all praise his bloodstained companions.
Lord, I myself shall praise Geraint,
An enemy to an Englishman, a friend to Christians.[210]

This last verse sets up an opposition between "Englishmen" and "Christians" which must go back to early days and may have coloured attitudes for a long time, in the pagan tyrant figures of Cornish drama for instance. Tradition maintained that Saint Petroc had fought in and survived the Battle of Camlann, Arthur's last battle, possibly at Camelford in Cornwall. These associations of early saints with independent Cornish kings and their wave of resistance may have helped to establish them as foci of national identity and founders of the early parish communities of Cornwall. The incomers may have been seen as "heathen" even after their conversion given that their saints and their church organization were so very different. As the historic identity of many saints fragmented with the passing of time their capacity to contain the projections and fantasies of their adherents may paradoxically have increased. Most importantly of course they offered the hope of salvation.

Other Irish saints came to Land's End and the Lizard,[211] and a Welsh/Breton group stopped in Cornwall on their journeys to and from, including Samson the famous Breton saint. A wave of Breton migrants arrived in the tenth century reversing the flight of their ancestors from Anglo-Saxon incursions five hundred years earlier. The cumulative impression gathered from all this to-ing and fro-ing is that early churchmen and perhaps the wider population to some extent regarded themselves as part of a wider Celtic world with linguistic, cultural, perhaps even family bonds which made freedom of movement seem natural. Although precise dating is rare, and the lives of the Cornish saints were lived long before Athelstan's conquest

---

210 See Rowland, J. (1990). *Early Welsh Saon Poetry*. Woodbridge, D. S. Brewer.
    Though the identity of the hero with the saint has been questioned.
211 See Doble, Part 2.

in the tenth century, and the country was not fully assimilated until much later, if at all.

Water and Stone

Cornish saints are often associated with holy wells, which were often converted into baptisteries in later centuries. Many wells seem to have been venerated in pre-Christian times and then incorporated into the new faith by the early saints, though some caused new springs to appear, as Meriasek does in the play:

> "Ihesu arluth me ath peys
> ihesu gront dovyr a wur speys
> ihesu dymmo der the graes
> del russys kyns the moyseys
> an men cales (ll. 667-70)

> Jesu, Lord, I beseech thee,
> Jesu, grant water in great abundance,
> Jesu, to me through thy grace
> As thou didst for Moses.
> From the hard rock."[212]

St Kea also prays to Christ for water and causes a well to spring up on his way to Rosewa.[213] Wells have always played an important role in Cornish life because of their saintly associations, their healing properties and their role in baptism, by means of which the newborn child is able to join the Christian community and obtain the sacraments which alone can procure salvation. As Hunt points out and the ritual of the church emphasizes:

> The purity of the fluid impresses itself, through the eye, upon the mind, and its power of removing all impurity is felt to the soil. "Wash and be clean" is the murmuring call of the waters, as they overflow their rocky basins or grassy vases: and deeply sunk in depravity must that man be who could put to unholy uses one of nature's fountains. The inner life

212 *Op. cit.*, pp.38-39.
213 See II 780-84.

of a well of water, bursting from its grave in the earth, may be religiously said to form a type of the soil purified by death, rising into a glorified existence and the fullness of light.[214]

and this spiritual quality has been recognized and channelled by people of different faiths and none. The sanctifying power of water was demonstrated at the well of St Constantine near Padstow. In a time of drought caused by the wickedness of the inhabitants the people turned to their priest for advice: he told them to clean the well but their lack of faith made them sceptical. When the drought persisted though they followed his advice. A cool stream flowed from the well, the sky clouded over and the rain poured down.

In another story Saint Ludgvan prayed and caused a magic spring to pour from the earth, and:

to try the virtues of the water, he washed his eyes. They were rendered at once more powerful, so penetrating indeed, as to enable him to see microscopic objects. The saint prayed again, and then he drank the water. He discovered that his powers of utterance were greatly improved, his tongue framed words with scarcely any effort of his will.[215]

In some ways this healing, inspirational water recalls the famous cauldron of Ceridiwen in Welsh tradition, drops from which were supposed to bestow wisdom and poetic inspiration on whoever drank them. The transformations of Ceridwen seem to be paralleled in the Breton stories of Koadalan, and the Korrigan, a seductive Breton fairy woman, which makes it possible that these tales were known in Cornwall. The Korrigan was associated with Wales, and Lewis Spence sees in her a "relation" of Saint Triduand of Restalrig in Scotland who presided over a well often visited by blind people: the water of Saint Ludgvan's well was said to protect the drinker from death by hanging. The Korrigan took babies, as the piskies sometimes did, leaving ugly changelings in their place, and also seduced unfortunate travellers in the forest, only to turn into a hideous old

214 Hunt, *op. cit.*, p. 285.
215 *Ibid.*, p. 288.

woman in the morning, reversing the transformation more usually found in folklore.[216]

Madron Well, near to Ludgvan parish, was the source of many miracles, and like other wells it attracted votive offerings in the shape of rags and pins attached to the bushes that surrounded the spring. In Madron churchyard is a short cross with the figure of Christ on the front, which seems to have been moved at some stage in its long life.[217] At Ludgvan churchyard is a taller cross which seems to be in its original position. Langdon tells us that

> Cornwall possesses a larger and more varied number of early Christian monuments than any other county (sic) in the British Isles.[218]

Even now Cornwall contains over three hundred crosses, and the number of surviving bases from which crosses have been removed suggests that there were once many more. Though crosses are often associated with churchyards, the majority are "dotted about in the bleak moor, and must have been, when erected originally far from any habitation". It seems that many of them were intended to show the way to the nearest church and to provide resting places for pallbearers. That

> the stone crosses were erected in order to disaffect and sanctify places which from time immemorial had been devoted to old pagan superstitions.[219]

seems likely on the evidence of the saints' lives. That of Saint Samson for instance, who encountered a pagan "idol" on his wanderings in Trigg. The saint performed a miracle, converted and baptized the bystanders and replaced the abominable image with a Christian symbol, and the narrator tells us:

216 Spence (no date, reprint 1997). *Legends and Romances: Brittany*. New York, Dover, pp. 59-60.
217 Langdon, A. G. (1988 reprint). *Old Cornish Crosses*. Exeter, Cornwall Books.
218 *Ibid*, p. 1.
219 Taylor, T. (1916). *The Celtic Christianity of Cornwall*. London, Longmans, p. 36.

"On this hill I myself have been and have adored and with my hand traced the sign of the cross which St Samson with his own hand carved by means of an iron instrument on a standing stone."[220]

As this makes clear, Samson's miracle and incision transforms the stone into a wayside cross, a focus for prayer and worship, a symbol of transformation. This process is paralleled by the transformation of pagan springs into holy wells, which was also effected by the saints, culminating in the sacrament of baptism itself, the most potent of transformations. An echo of this paradigmatic shift survives perhaps in the later use of pagan burial mounds as theatres for portraying the death and resurrection of Christ. This paradox embodying the tension between continuity and change is at the heart of Cornish culture. And in all three of these domains the saint plays a central role, both as messenger from another world and representative of the community and its cultural heritage.

Relics

In medieval Europe the saint was often felt to be physically present through his relics, fragments of bone or objects associated with him in life, which were thought to possess something of his spiritual power. This belief survives in the Catholic world where relics provide a focus for prayer and reflection, though the sale of relics became a scandal which helped to precipitate the Reformation. The possession of relics conferred status and legitimacy on religious institutions by demonstrating a link with the founder or the wellsprings of the Faith. It also generated income from the faithful and this increased the temptation to abuse, though the extent of this may have been overstated: the Reformer John Calvin was fond of claiming that there were enough alleged fragments of the True Cross, upon which Christ was crucified, to fill a cargo ship, but research by Charles Rohovest de Fleury, who catalogued all known fragments of the True Cross, has shown that together they would make up only one tenth of a whole cross.[221] For a believer though contact with such a relic would connect him or her with the sacred history of Christ's

220 Taylor, T. (1925), *op. cit.*, p. 49.
221 See Curti, E. (2016). 'The Dating Game'. *The Tablet 9/1/16*. pp.8-9.

Passion, and historical authenticity is not really the issue. Though often characterized as peasant superstition this actually represents a much more sophisticated way of apprehending the world than the shallow positivism of our own time, a vision which, like Blake's can embrace both the superficial appearance of everyday life and the transcendent reality which underlies it.

An inventory of the relics of St Piran survives from the year 1281. It includes the head of the saint in its reliquary (reliquaries were often beautiful, costly portable shrines, in which the parts of the saint's body were placed for processions), teeth from St Brendan and Saint Martin in a silver box, and St Piran's own pastoral staff decorated with gold, silver and precious stones. Saint Brendan was the famous voyager with whom Piran was often associated. The procession was a public display, an act of memory and celebration, as it still is in Brittany:

> From far and wide the people crowd to this festival, which is one of the most extraordinary in Brittany. Down every dark street flowed a double file of lights, each casting a bright reflection on the face of the person who bore it. Thus, most of the pilgrims being in black and their bodies not distinguishable from the darkness, it seemed a procession of white-capped, white-winged cherubs, of various ages, floating in mid-air, while in their midst appeared rich banners, reliquaries, statues of favourite saints and finally "Madame Marie de Bon Secours" (the Virgin Mary) herself, in embroidered satin and sparkling, jewelled crown.[222]

Petroc's Unquiet Bones

The importance of relics is underlined by an incident which took place in 1177 when the body of St Petroc was stolen from Bodmin and taken to the monastery of St Meen in Brittany. The thief, a canon of Saint Petroc's priory seems to have had a grievance against the house and had been disciplined by the prior. St Meen or Mewan had been a disciple of Saint Samson, who played an important part in the story of Petroc, who was also revered at St Meen as well as in

222 Gostling, F. M (1909). *The Bretons at Home*. London, Methuen and Co, p. 23.

Bodmin and parts of Wales. He has dedications in Devon and Somerset too and Doble tells us: "it is clear that Petroc was the apostle of the whole of the kingdom of Dumnonia", that is the old Celtic kingdom of the southwest. Petroc gave his name to Padstow, and seems to have come originally from Wales where he came from royal stock and had a reputation as a war-leader. In Welsh tradition he was "Petroc Baladrddellt" ("Splintered Spear"), one of the "Tri Chyvion Varchoc", the "Three Just Knights" of Arthur's court, and a survivor of Camlann.[223] He is thus linked to the period of heroic struggle against the Saxon invaders, though he eventually renounced war and became a priest. Petroc refuses to become king when his parents die, much as Meriasek refuses to marry the Armorican princess in order to be consecrated a knight of God. Though the beginning of *Bewnans Ke* is missing, Albert Le Grand's *Life* of the saint describes his renunciation of Episcopal authority in order to become a hermit: Kea too was of noble birth "in the Isle of Britain".[224] Each of these men renounced power and wealth in his own world to make a voyage, a voyage of spiritual discovery and transformation.

The *De reliquarum furto*, a Bodmin manuscript concerning the theft of the relics, describes their importance in promoting the reputation of the saint. In another account, the "Miracula", various miracles are attributed to the relics.[225] In one of these a Cornish sailor invokes Petroc to calm a storm, in another episode, not strictly speaking miraculous, the Bodmin canons use the relics to avert what they perceive to be unjust taxation. At this point the relics apparently included an ivory horn given to Petroc by King Constantine when he was converted to Christianity. Constantine was an early Cornish king, mentioned by Gildas as the "tyrant whelp of the filthy lioness of Dumnonia", who abdicated and became an abbot.[226]

Though Martin seems to have stolen the relics for personal reasons the Breton monks clearly hoped to make use of them as Bodmin had done to strengthen their own legitimacy and use their powers for both spiritual and worldly ends. The channels of communication

---

223 Jankulak, K. (2000). *The Medieval Cult of Saint Petroc*. Woodbridge, Boydell and Brewer, p. 13.

224 Thomas and Williams, *op. cit.*, xii.

225 Jankulak, *op. cit.*, p. 17.

226 Deacon, op. cit., p. 6.

between Brittany and Cornwall made the theft relatively easy, and these channels had played an important part in the life of the saint centuries earlier, just as the miracles performed by the power of the relics recapitulate the miracles performed by the saint in life. They also raise the questions of legitimacy, justice and possession which play a large part in the Cornish drama, and in Cornish history, in the genesis of the 1497 rebellion for instance.

The *De reliquarum furto* also contains the theory that the theft was a punishment for the sins of the Bodmin priors. The theft itself was not known at Bodmin until reports of the miracles worked by the relics reached Cornwall from Brittany, which does seem somewhat casual. Though the motives for the theft were supposed to be demonic the author takes the view "that the theft was necessary to make Petroc known throughout and beyond Cornwall". The relics were offered to the Count of Brittany to strengthen his claim to be the legitimate ruler of Cornwall, for:

> If that body of the most holy confessor (i.e. Petroc) were kept safely and carefully, the whole of Cornwall would soon be subjected to the county of Brittany, of his lord, the son of the king of England.[227]

Even dead saints, it seemed, could confer legitimacy. Of course, the author has his own agenda, and Martin's real motives remain obscure. The narrator is ambivalent about that, while inferring that, though Martin was an opportunistic liar, he may have had a

> greater agenda (to join Cornwall and Brittany under the proper lordship of (Count) Geoffrey. Martin has now moved from being a spiteful malcontent to acting as an agent of larger issues of political authority, unity and justice.[228]

When the Bodmin authorities heard the news, they enlisted the help of powerful noblemen with Cornish connections, such as Richard de Lucy and Walter of Coutances. They then appealed to King Henry II who also ruled Brittany at the time, who ordered the

227 Jankulak, op. cit., p. 23.
228 *Ibid.*, p. 24.

restoration of the relics to Bodmin, and a party was sent to retrieve them. We never hear what happens to Martin.

This story illustrates many things: the personal nature of politics in the twelfth century, the rivalry between ecclesiastical authorities at that time (as we also saw in the case of Glastonbury and Arthur's spurious grave); among them, as well as the enduring connectedness between Brittany and Cornwall, and the role of the saints in strengthening that bond. Even when dead saints were potential agents of transformation capable of reuniting the divided peoples of ancient Dumnonia in a new Brythonic kingdom, it was not to be and remains another of Cornwall's great might have beens, like Richard Grenville's independent Cornwall under the king. But this was the background against which the saints of Cornwall became a focus for Cornish identity, as Arthur had once been. The saint's life was the point at which Christianity entered Cornwall and began to shape its history, just as Christ in person entered it in the legend of the Holy Visit, opening up the possibilities of a new world, as Blake the visionary saw.

The stories of Cornwall—the tale of Arthur, of Tristan and Iseult, as well as the legends told by the common people and the ancient drama—come down to us from an unimaginably distant past. They have helped the Cornish people to sustain their identity through the darkest times, to reach out to their neighbours in the wider world, and to hope for a future in which they can be themselves.

Bibliography

Angarrack, J. (1999). *Breaking the Chains: Propaganda, Deception and the Manipulation of Public Opinion in Cornwall*. Camborne, Cornish Stannary Publications.

Ashe, G. (ed.) Reprinted (1979). *The Quest for Arthur's Britain*. London, Paladin.

Bakere, J. A. (1980). *The Cornish Ordinalia: A Critical Study*. Cardiff, University of Wales Press.

Barczewski, S. (2000). *Myth and National Identity in Nineteenth Century Britain*. Oxford, Oxford University Press.

Baring-Gould, S. (1899). *A Book of Cornwall*. London, Methuen.

Barton, R. M. (1997). *Life in Cornwall in the Early Nineteenth Century*. Redruth, Truran.

Bédier, J. (1973). (trans. H. Belloc). The Romance of Tristan and Iseult. New York, Random House.

Berresford-Ellis, P. (1974). *The Cornish Language and its Literature*. London, Routledge and Kegan Paul.

Briggs, K. (1976). *A Dictionary of Fairies*. London, Penguin.

Bromwich, R. (ed.) 4th edition (2014). *Trioedd Ynys Prydein: The Triads of the Island of Britain*. Cardiff, University of Wales Press.

Broome, D. (1951). *Fairy Tales from the Isle of Man*. Douglas, Norris Press.

Burgess, G. (ed.) (1975). *Chrétien de Troyes: Arthurian Romances*. London, Dent.

Busby, K. (ed.) (1986). *The Lais of Marie de France*. London, Penguin.

Carew, R. (2000). *Survey of Cornwall 1602*. Redruth, Tamar Books.

Carney, J. (1955). *Studies in Irish Literature and History*. Dublin, Dublin Institute of Advanced Studies.

Carson, C. (2007). *The Táin*. London, Penguin.

Coleman, W. (2015). *Plen An Gwari. The Playing Places of Cornwall*. Golden Tree.

Courtney, M. A. (1886). Reprinted (1998). *Cornish Feasts and Folklore*. Penzance, Oakmagic.

Cross, T. P. and Slover, C. H. (eds.) (1936). Reprinted (1996). *Ancient Irish Tales*. New York, Barnes and Noble.

Cunliffe, B. (2011). *Europe Between the Oceans: 9000 B.C.-A.D.1000*. New Haven, Yale University Press.

Deacon, B. (2007). *Cornwall: A Concise History*. Cardiff, University of Wales Press.

Deane, T. and Shaw, T. (2003). *Folklore of Cornwall*. Stroud, Tempus.

Doble, G. H.(1931). Reprinted (1997). *The Saints of Cornwall I-VI*. Felinfach, Llanerch Press.

Dobson, C. C. (1936). *Did Our Lord Visit Britain as They Say in Cornwall and Somerset?* Glastonbury, Avalon Press.

BIBLIOGRAPHY

Drabble, M. (ed.) Revised 6th edition (2006). *The Oxford Companion to English Literature*. Oxford, Oxford University Press.

Eisner, S. (1969). *The Tristan Legend: A Study in Sources*. Evanston, North Western University Press.

Enright, M. (1996). *Lady with a Mead Cup: Ritual, Prophesy and Lordship in the European Warband*. Dublin, Four Courts Press.

Fedrick, A. S. (trans.) (1970). *The Romance of Tristan by Béroul*. London, Penguin.

Giot *et al* (2008). *The British Settlement of Brittany*. Stroud, Tempus.

Gostling (1909). *The Bretons at Home*. London, Methuen.

Gowans, L. M. (1988). 'Cei and the Arthurian Legend', *Arthurian Studies xviii*. Cambridge, D. S. Brewer.

Halliday, F. E. (1955). *The Legend of the Rood*. London, Duckworth.

Hamilton Jenkin, A. K. (1927). *The Cornish Miner*. London, Allen and Unwin.

Harman, A. and Milner, A. (1983). *Late Renaissance Art: Baroque Music*.

Harris, M. (1962). *The Cornish Ordinalia: A Critical Study*. Washington, Catholic University of America.

Henchen, H. O. (1922). *The Archaeology of Cornwall and Scilly*. London, Methuen and Co.

Higham, J. (2002). *King Arthur: Myth-Making and History*. London, Routledge.

Hunt, R., 3rd edition (1881). *Popular Romances of the West of England*. London, Chatto and Windus.

Hutton, R. (2003). *Witches Druids and King Arthur*. London, Bloomsbury.

Jankulak, K. (2000). *The Medieval Cult of Saint Petroc*. Woodbridge, Boydell and Brewer.

Jarman, A. O. H. (ed.) (1988). *Aneirin: Y Gododdin*. Llandysol, Gomer Press.

Jenner, H. (1904). *A Handbook of the Cornish Language*. London, David Nutt. Revised edition (2010), ed. Michael Everson. Cathair na Mart: Evertype.

Jones, G. and Jones, T. (1948) Reprinted (1970). *The Mabinogion*. London, Dent.

Kent, A. (2000). *The Literature of Cornwall: Continuity, Identity, Difference 1000-2000*. Bristol, Redcliffe.

Kent, A. (2010). *The Theatre of Cornwall: Space, Place, Performance*. Bristol, Redcliffe/Westcliffe Books.

Kinsella, T. (1970). *The Táin*. London, Oxford University Press.

Knight, S. (1983). *Arthurian Literature and Society*. London, MacMillan.

Korrel, P (1984). *An Arthurian Triangle: A Study of the Origin, Development and Characterisation of Arthur, Guinevere and Modred*. Leiden, E. J. Brill.

Kristeva, J. (1989). *Black Sun*. New York, Columbia University Press.

Langdon, A. G. Reprinted (1988). *Old Cornish Crosses*. Exeter, Cornwall Books

Laplanche, J. and Pontalis, J. B. (1973). *The Language of Psychoanalysis*. London, Hogarth Press.

Lewis, H. A. (no date). *Christ in Cornwall?* Falmouth, J. H. Lake.

Lewis, L. S. (1922). *Saint Joseph of Arimathea at Glastonbury*. Wells, Clare and Son.

Lewis, T. (ed.) (1966). *Geoffrey of Monmouth: The History of the Kings of Britain.* Harmondsworth, Penguin.

Loomis, R. S. (1926). Reprinted (1993*). Celtic Myth and Arthurian Romance.* London, Constable.

McKillop, J. (1998). *Dictionary of Celtic Mythology.* Oxford, Oxford University Press.

McMahon, B. (2016). *Gathering the Fragments: Storytelling and Cultural Resistance in Cornwall.* Portlaoise, Evertype.

Malory, T. (1996). *Le Morte d'Arthur.* Ware, Wordsworth.

Mathews, J. and Stewart, R. J. (1995). *Merlin Through the Ages.* London, Blandford.

Megaw, R. and Megaw, V. (1997). "Do the Ancient Celts Still Exist? An Essay on Identity and Contextuality." *Studia Celtica 31*, pp. 107-28.

Mersey, D. (2004). *Arthur King of the Britons: From Celtic Hero to Cinema Icon.* Chichester, Summersdale.

Meyer, K. (ed.) (1895). Reprinted (1994). *The Voyage of Bran.* Felinfach, Llanarch.

Morris, J. (1973). *The Age of Arthur. A History of the British Isles from 350 to 650 A. D.* London, Weidenfeld and Nicholson.

Murdoch, B. (1993). *Cornish Literature.* Woodbridge, D. S. Brewer.

Myres, J. N. L. (1986). *The English Settlements.* Oxford, Clarendon Press.

Ní Shéaghdha, N. (ed.) (1967). *Tóruigheacht Dhiarmada agus Ghráinne: The Pursuit of Diarmaid and Gráinne.* Dublin, Irish Texts Society.

Norris, E. (ed. and trans.) (1859). *The Ancient Cornish Drama.* Oxford, Oxford University Press.

O'Donaghue, D. (1893). Reprinted (1994). *Lives and Legends of St Brendan.* Fellinfach, Llanerch.

O'Keefe, J. G. (1913). *Buile Suibne: Being the Adventures of Suibhne Geilt, A Middle Irish Romance.* London, Irish Texts Society.

Ó Tuama, S. (1981). 'The Lineage of Gaelic Love Poetry from the Earliest Times.' In O'Driscoll, R. (ed.) (1982). *The Celtic Consciousness.* New York, George Braziller.

Owen, D. D. R. (ed.) (1975). *Chrétien de Troyes: Arthurian Romances.* London, J. M. Dent.

Padel, O. J. (1981). 'The Cornish Background of the Tristan Stories'. *Cambridge Medieval Celtic Studies 1*, pp.53-81.

Pascoe, W. H. (1985). *Teudar—A King of Cornwall.* Redruth, Dyllansow Truran.

Payton, P. (1992). 'A Concealed Envy against the English, A Note on the Aftermath of the 1497 rebellions in Cornwall.' In Payton, P. (ed.) (1992). *Cornish Studies 6.*

Payton, P. (1992). *The Making of Modern Cornwall.* Redruth, Dyllansow Truran.

Payton, P. (2004). *Cornwall: A History.* Fowey, Cornwall Editions.

Quiller-Couch, A. and Du Maurier, D. (1962). Reprinted (1979). *Castle Dor.* London, Pan Books.

BIBLIOGRAPHY

Quinn, E. C. (1962). *The Quest of Seth for the Oil of Life*. Chicago, Chicago University Press.

Rees, A. and Rees, R. (1961). *Celtic Heritage*. London, Thames and Hudson.

Rolleston, T. W. (1911). *Myths and Legends of the Celtic Race*. London, Harrap and Co.

Rowe, J. Reprinted (1993). *Cornwall in the Age of the Industrial Revolution*. St Austell, Cornish Hillside Publications.

Rowland, J. (1990). *Early Welsh Saga Poetry*. Woodbridge, D. S. Brewer.

Schoepperle, G. (1913). Reprinted New York (1959). *Tristan and Isolt: A Study of the Sources of the Romance*. Frankfurt and London.

Seddon, R. (1990). *The Mystery of Arthur at Tintagel*. London, Rudolf Steiner Press.

Spence, L. (1948). *The Minor Traditions of British Mythology*. London, Rider and Co.

Spence, L. Reprinted (1997). Legends and Romances of Brittany. New York, Dover.

Stoyle, M. (2002). *West Britons: Cornish Identities and the Early Modern British State*, Exeter, University of Exeter Press.

Stoyle, M. (2005). *Soldiers and Strangers: An Ethnic History of the English Civil War*. New Haven, Yale University Press.

Symons, A. C. (2003). Quiller-Couch on Tristan and Ysyllt. *An Baner Kernewek* 112.

Taylor, T. (1916). *The Celtic Christianity of Cornwall*. London, Longmans.

Thomas, C. (1981). *Christianity in Roman Britain*. London, B. T. Batsford.

Thomas, C. (1994). *And Shall These Mute Stones Speak? Post-Roman Inscriptions in Western Britain*. Cardiff, University of Wales Press.

Thomas, G. and Williams, N. (2007). *Bewnans Ke*. Exeter, Exeter University Press.

Thomas, P. W. and Williams, D. (eds.) (2007). *Setting Cornwall on its Feet: Robert Morton Nance 1873-1959*. London, Francis Boutle.

Thompson, S. (1977). *The Folktale*. Berkeley, University of California Press.

Trotter, L (2012). 'Husband Abroad'. *Cornish Studies 20*. Payton, P (ed.).

Von Strassburg, G. (1960). *Tristan*. London, Penguin.

Westwood, J. (1985). *Albion: A Guide to Legendary Britain*. London, Granada.

Westwood, J. and Simpson, J. (2005). *The Lore of the Land*. London, Penguin.

William of Malmesbury. Reprinted 1908). *The Antiquities of Glastonbury*. Felinfach, Llanerch.

Williams, D. R. (2004). *Henry and Katherine Jenner*. London, Francis Boutle.

Index

www.ingramcontent.com/pod-product-compliance
Lightning Source LLC
Chambersburg PA
CBHW031211270326
41931CB00006B/520